Advance Praise for *Real Impact*

"Morgan Simon has made a significant contribution with the very big idea that we can change the world by changing how we all relate to money. And lucky for us, Simon is as entertaining in her writing as she is brilliant in her concepts."   —VAN JONES, CNN

"Impact investing is a subject that deserves in-depth, powerful scrutiny. [Simon] gives readers an introduction into understanding where this kind of work can bring hopeful change and where it can't. Timely!"   —BILL MCKIBBEN, author of *Deep Economy*

"Where we invest speaks to our values as a country that prioritizes our collective social welfare. Morgan Simon's innovative investment approach ensures money can serve as a force for good, for everyone."

—CONGRESSMAN KEITH ELLISON, member of the
House Financial Services Committee and
co-chair, Congressional Progressive Caucus

"*Real Impact* is a unique and valuable teaching tool. Morgan Simon's expertise in the field is unparalleled, and brilliantly shared through this book."

—VIKRAM GANDHI, senior lecturer, Harvard
Business School, and former vice-chairman
of investment banking, Credit Suisse

"To drive significant social and environmental progress around the world, investors need to understand how to structure and deliver capital in a way that works for high-impact enterprises. *Real Impact* highlights the complicated trade-offs they will face along the risk–return spectrum and offers a blueprint for market growth. It helps fill the knowledge gap between optimism and execution."

—DEBRA D. SCHWARTZ, managing director of
impact investments, MacArthur Foundation

"A critical cautionary tale—how do we scale social impact investment without leaving anyone behind? Morgan Simon is a master practitioner at inclusive investment; read *Real Impact* to learn from her compelling example."

—BEN JEALOUS, partner, Kapor Capital,
and former president, NAACP

"*Real Impact* is a gift to the academic community. I know of no other resource available with such a balance of thought-provoking investment philosophy and practical advice—reflecting the depth of Morgan Simon's expertise and experience in impact investment."

—HEIDI KRAUEL PATEL, lecturer in management,
Graduate School of Business at Stanford University

"Over 1,700 asset owners around the world, from pension funds to insurance companies and sovereign wealth funds, have become signatories to the UNPRI, as it becomes increasingly clear that social and environmental trends can create financial opportunities. Investors now have the capacity to help solve the world's problems and deliver strong returns for their beneficiaries and clients. Morgan Simon is a global leader in impact investing, and this book offers critical lessons for those interested in being on the cutting edge of this exciting new field."

—DR. JAMES GIFFORD, founder and former executive director, United
Nations Principles on Responsible Investment,
and senior impact investment strategist, UBS

"Global development organizations looking for sustainable models are increasingly turning to impact investment as the wave of the future. At times, we have reasonable skepticism about whether investing will ultimately contribute to, or end poverty. Morgan Simon lays out an inspiring roadmap that shows how we can harness this tool for good to its highest purpose."

—MICHELLE NUNN, president and CEO, CARE USA

REAL
IMPACT

The New Economics
of Social Change

Morgan Simon

NATION BOOKS
NEW YORK

Published in the United States by Nation Books, an imprint of Perseus Books, LLC, a subsidiary of Hachette Book Group, Inc.

Nation Books is a co-publishing venture of the Nation Institute and Perseus Books

The author, Morgan Simon, does not offer specific investment recommendations or advice to the reader of this material, which is general in nature and should not be considered a comprehensive review or analysis of the topics discussed. This material is intended to be impersonal in nature and does not take into account the individual circumstances of readers or any institutions they may represent.

A reader should not make personal financial or investment decisions based solely upon reading this material. This material is not a substitute for or the same as a consultation with an investment advisor in a one-on-one context whereby all the facts of the reader's situation can be considered in its entirety and the investment advisor can provide individualized investment advice or a customized financial plan. Financial planning and investment strategies have the potential for loss, and investment advisors cannot offer any guarantees or promises of success. Despite efforts to be accurate and current, this material may contain out-of-date information; the author will not be under an obligation to advise the reader of any subsequent changes related to the topics discussed in this material.

The author is not an attorney or an accountant and does not provide legal, tax, or accounting advice. The author recommends that each reader should take time to research investment advisor firms, investment advisor representatives, and the services and products being offered before establishing an investment advisory relationship with any firm or making any investments.

Books published by Nation Books are available at special discounts for bulk purchases in the United States by corporations, institutions, and other organizations.

Designed by Linda Mark

Library of Congress Cataloging-in-Publication Data
Names: Simon, Morgan, author.
Title: Real impact : the new economics of social change / Morgan Simon.
Description: First Edition. | New York : Nation Books, 2017.
Identifiers: LCCN 2017005419 (print) | LCCN 2017020982 (ebook) |
ISBN 9781568589817 (ebook) | ISBN 9781568589800 (hardback)
Subjects: LCSH: Charities. | Investments, Foreign—Moral and ethical aspects.
| Economic development. | Social responsibility of business. | Social change. |
BISAC: SOCIAL SCIENCE / Philanthropy & Charity. | BUSINESS & ECONOMICS /
Nonprofit Organizations & Charities.
Classification: LCC HV40 (ebook) | LCC HV40 .S58667 2017 (print) | DDC
361.7/6—dc23
LC record available at https://lccn.loc.gov/2017005419

LSC-C

10 9 8 7 6 5 4 3 2 1

Dedicated to Janet Shenk

CONTENTS

INTRODUCTION

Getting Real

LET'S START BY GETTING REAL HERE.

Real is the harm that the global economy has caused through centuries of extractive practices.

Real are the challenges that decades of ineffective charitable work have caused in covering up structural economic problems that ensure the persistence of poverty and inequity.

Real is the potential for a new field called impact investment—the practice of investing not just for profit, but also for social benefit—to completely restructure the global economy, making social and environmental responsibility integral to how we move money through society, rather than an afterthought.

Real is the fact that impact investment is already being done on a massive scale by a limited number of people. It's the trillion-dollar trend most people have never heard of.

Real is the fact that impact investment is in danger of replicating the same mistakes of the aid industry by focusing on palliative rather than structural change, and by choosing outside "experts" as its leaders, rather than responding more to those whose expertise is grounded in a lived reality.

Real is the opportunity we have to get this right. We can transform the way impact investment has often been practiced, scaling interventions that actually create long-term, systemic impact and that stay accountable to the communities they aim to serve.

Every generation lives on the cusp of major social transformations. Ours is witnessing revolutionary changes in the role of capital in society, with trillions of dollars migrating toward positive social and environmental purposes. It would be a tragedy to let this moment pass without attempting to maximize its potential as conscious consumers of impact investment. In this book I offer a framework that I hope will inspire and guide us to real, world-changing impact, and share some of the stories of the people and communities that have inspired me.

Social change is a process in which people—perfectly imperfect as we are—work together to create better outcomes. Though our efforts often fall short, we are still responsible for doing the best we can. *Real Impact* is my attempt to do my part by providing a roadmap for people who are interested in engaging in the practice of impact investment with integrity and accountability—and in a way that really solves problems for the long term.

I have spent the past seventeen years working at the intersection of finance and social justice, building four leading organizations in the field—the Responsible Endowments Coalition,

Toniic, Pi Investments, and Transform Finance—that collectively seek to influence how and where over \$150 billion is invested. In 2016 we began also supporting the Libra Foundation in their impact investment journey in addition to supporting Pi Investments. We work in deep relationship with the two families behind these efforts, taking advantage of their aligned values to support both in building portfolios with a commitment to social justice and in alignment with the Transform Finance principles.

These experiences have given me a unique perspective on the practice of impact investment—but I by no means claim to have all the answers. The approach we take at Transform Finance, the organization I cofounded to build a bridge between social justice and impact investment, is to focus predominantly on making sure the industry asks the right questions, knowing that it will take a broad community and the lessons of experience over time to answer these questions effectively. In these pages, I share what I've learned as well as the questions we should continue to ask ourselves as we develop this powerful new vehicle for social change and aim to ensure that our impact is real: transformative, not palliative.*

What will it take to make impact investment truly transformative? One of our greatest resources is the intellectual capital of the world's people. On the one hand, we have frontline communities and activists who share a deep understanding of the costs of doing business as usual and a vision of what social

---

*The word *palliative* is most often heard in the context of palliative care, but it could apply as well to social impact endeavors. Its more general definition, according to *Merriam-Webster*, is "to ease (symptoms) without curing the underlying disease."

and environmental harmony might look like. On the other, we have experienced practitioners in the investment community who know how to bring together large amounts of capital and effectively leverage it toward a goal. If we put these two forces together and develop new structures to ensure that they share power equitably, we will have a much better chance of building an economy that is generative and just.

Impact investing is at an inflection point. If we are going to ensure it's on the right path, it's going to take some hard work from activists and investors alike. Indeed, it's going to take collaborations between two communities that rarely come together, with structural innovation to facilitate joint efforts and the effective sharing of power. Practically and philosophically, we need each other, and once we establish mutual objectives and practical structures for working together, we might very well appreciate each other's company, too.

Anyone, not just professional organizers and investors, can play a role in changing the economic equation and bringing about a more just and equitable world, as we all participate in the global economy. To help guide a diverse readership on their journey toward a new economics of social change, here is a brief summary of the book's organization.

In Chapters 1 and 2, I share my experience as an idealistic activist eager to play a part in rectifying social injustice and struggling to find the right way to engage with the world. After a brief stint in international development, I began to recognize the limitations of charity as a vehicle for long-term structural change. I discovered that investment—and, in particular, the new field of impact investment—was an incredibly powerful and underutilized tool for creating a more generative and just world. In these chapters I also provide historical background on the field, introduce some definitions, and encourage both skeptics and supporters to think more deeply about the potential of impact investment.

As I made my first forays into the impact investment world, however, I also saw that though most investments were being made with the very good intention of adding social and environmental value, many were ultimately limited in their impact—eradicating the symptoms but not the disease. Projects may have succeeded in making the poor a little and momentarily better off, but did not address the overall power imbalance of the global economy. In Chapters 3 and 4, I examine why impact investment so often fails to maximize its potential. A related form of investment, microfinance, began as a Nobel Prize–winning idea for fighting poverty, but as it scaled it went astray and lost much of its impact. There are lessons we can learn from its trajectory. Impact investment is at a similar pivotal point—preparing to scale rapidly, but in need of structural guidelines to ensure that the impact will rise in adequate proportion to the increase in dollars deployed.

Current practitioners may find some of the analysis in these early chapters to be rather pointed. And they are right. My intention, however, is always to create greater awareness of the flaws in the system we have collectively created, not to point fingers at individual parties. Anyone who gets involved in impact work does so with the best of intentions, and I provide this critique only to encourage all of us to channel those good intentions into institutional and procedural reforms—reforms that, in part, will broaden our community of practice, and in turn facilitate more truly impactful investments.

Most of this book focuses on potential solutions to the problems I describe, and on the opportunity we have to scale something truly transformative. The critique is simply fuel for the fire of new ideas and opportunities.

Chapter 5 proposes a new model for impact investment and a set of principles that might enable it to actualize its potential not only to create wealth, but to produce systemic economic, political, and social change. I describe how these principles—the Transform Finance principles—were developed, in a dialogue between investors and communities, and how they can effectively guide the movement.

Chapters 6 through 9 tell stories of specific impact investment projects that bring these principles to life. A few are recounted because they exemplify what exactly goes awry when investors do "business as usual," but many more are inspiring success stories showing the profound progress that we can achieve—and the ways both investors and communities can gain—when the Transform Finance principles are put into action.

Chapter 10 continues to move from principles to practices, sharing our work with Pi Investments. On behalf of a member of the Pritzker family, we helped build a portfolio that seeks transformative change with 100 percent of assets across different types of investments, from private equity to real assets. This chapter should be particularly illuminating for investors and institutions such as foundations and family offices that are engaged in the process of exploring questions such as "What kind of impact do we want to have, and why?" and "How can we structure this into a full portfolio, with sensitivity to both financial and impact return targets?"

Finally, Chapter 11 addresses the reader who may not work in the investment field, but does want to leverage the power each of us has to bring about change through our everyday interactions with the economy—from where we do our banking to how our retirement savings are invested, from what kind of businesses or organizations we want to help create to how our social movements can produce earned income or engage in economic activism.

I invite readers to use this book as an opportunity to reflect deeply on what having real impact can mean to your work. If you are an aspiring impact investor or social entrepreneur, how can you best support transformative change? How will you establish personal and professional practices to keep accountable to social movements and frontline communities? What does best practice really look like—and how can it look different from previous, failed models?

I hope that asking such questions will enable you to look back at your career in thirty years with confidence that you truly made a positive, sustainable, systemic change in the world and didn't just choose easy Band-Aid solutions, replicating the mistakes of traditional charity that impact investment was designed to correct. Replicating past mistakes is all too easy, because the conventional financial system automatically gives us the power—even encourages us—to make exactly the wrong decisions. Building a more balanced approach in the context of impact investment will require a different way of thinking about process, expertise, and partnerships. In this book I outline new approaches to these essential building blocks that I hope will lead to better outcomes for all, including a more exciting and meaningful professional life for everyone in the field.

If you are an activist or change-maker-at-large, no matter what your issue—racial justice, food access, climate change, housing, gender, income inequality, or all of the above—I'm sure you're all too aware that economic forces have a major impact on everyday people and the planet. I invite you to use this book as an accessible guide to engaging with the financial world—a world that is making decisions to the detriment of the communities and landscapes you care about every single day—and to leveraging its power for social transformation.

The Transform Finance approach is not an attempt to "dismantle the master's house with the master's tools," to quote the writer and activist Audre Lorde; rather, it is aligned with this statement by philosopher Frantz Fanon: "I, the man of color, want only this: That the tool never possess the man." It is an invitation to use money in a new way to build a new economy, leveraging the traditional practices of commerce, trade, and investment to replace assets stolen from global communities over the course of history. Sure, engaging in the economy can sometimes feel dirty and complicated, and it may invoke negative feedback from peers who perceive such work as less radical. But to ignore this opportunity would be to turn our backs on the communities that must deal with the daily consequences of the economy as it is—the economy in which we all implicitly participate. We have an opportunity to convert the economy into a tool that works for all of us, and into an effective mechanism of change for the people and communities it has left behind for far too long.

At this unique moment in history, we have the opportunity, working together, to create structures that will rebuild an economy to serve real people and foster a healthier planet. With this book, I hope to inspire social activists to take a fresh look at the power of capital to inform powerful and positive social, economic, and environmental changes. I want to urge aspiring impact investors to take up the challenge of building a better industry encompassing a broad and inclusive community, one that refuses to settle for anything less than transformative change. That is my invitation to you—to take this journey together. It will be messy, challenging, heartbreaking, intense, and beautiful—and it will be well worth our collective effort.

one

THE LIMITS OF CHARITY

I WAS BORN AND RAISED IN THE UNITED STATES, A COUN-try founded on the intellectual assumption that free markets are the most efficient allocators of resources to support society. A corollary of this assumption is that the best way to correct market or personal failures is through government subsidies and charitable donations. One works to earn a living, and then uses free time to participate in the classic American pastime of "helping the less fortunate." Our economy works the same way: it generates substantial value, and then some percentage of whatever is deemed to be extra, whether at an individual or corporate level, is what gets allocated toward helping others.

I don't know if I fully believed or even perceived this paradigm on a conscious level when, as a teenager, I channeled my youthful anger at the world's social structure into volunteering, thinking this was the thing one does when one wants to help people. Upon high school graduation I was tied with

my friend Jamie Long for having logged more community service hours than any other student in our class of 274. I spent
so much time doing service in part because I deeply enjoyed
the relationships I built in the process of working largely with
immigrant families in downtown Los Angeles. When I went
to "do volunteer work," I felt like I was just going to hang
out with friends: people who were important to me. I also felt
genuinely angry that these people I cared about didn't have the
same access as I did to education, secure housing, quality jobs,
or the general bounty of the American economy.

I saw that markets were failing people over and over again,
particularly people who looked or spoke a certain way. But I
didn't give up on the idea that the right intervention through
the nonprofit sector, or via public policy, could fix the problem, and that these channels were the source of a solution. It
took me a decade of experience before that belief fully unrav-
eled; before I came to realize that these "good works" were
actually part of the problem in legitimizing an inequitable economic system.

It isn't news that this free-market-plus-charity model is failing to produce global prosperity and well-being. Its failure is
why we seek out new solutions like impact investment. But
I've only recently begun to see how our unconscious cultural
attitudes toward the economy actually shape what we view as
possible. There must be another way to structure an economy
to better serve people, if only we can access the imagination
required to envision it.

For those of us in the United States, for instance, it can
be hard to imagine an alternative to the kind of capitalism
we're used to. Or for us to understand and appreciate local
economic structures, such as cooperatives, that are common

and successful across the Global South but rarely used here. Throughout my career I have spent time in forty-seven different countries, including some—as wide ranging as the Netherlands, Brazil, Cuba, and Sweden—with economic views that are very different from our own. I do not raise this point to invoke the classic capitalism-versus-socialism argument, but just to say I know it's incredibly hard for *all* sides of that debate to break out of their respective worldviews and try to envision new rules for a global economy. Engaging with this book may require an unlearning, an openness to the idea that we can learn from strategies that do not immediately seem to fit our preconceived notions, so that ultimately we can use this knowledge to build a very different economic system.

Envisioning alternatives does not mean that charity and aid are universally bad; clearly they have the potential to do good. Instead, it's recognizing that they are structurally inefficient in creating systemic change, in part because they themselves are integral to the current system. Ultimately, they unwittingly reinforce the economic paradigms that provide people with fundamentally unequal access to both resources and opportunity.

We will get into the macro-mechanics by which this happens—but first, I want to share how a can of tuna provoked my final crisis of confidence about aid and charity and helped me avoid years of work propping up a failing system.

A CAN OF WORMS: ENOUGH IS ENOUGH

It was the summer of 2003. I was twenty years old and working in Sierra Leone under the auspices of the Special Court, the United Nations–sponsored body charged with trying to make sense of the ten-year civil war in that country. I was an economics and political science major at Swarthmore College, obsessed with the development field and dreaming of my eventual posting, perhaps under the auspices of USAID or the United Nations itself.

I had been matched with a local nonprofit called Green Scenery, led by Ashoka Fellow Joseph Rahall. My task was to evaluate, and suggest improvements to, a government-sponsored tree-planting program that had been recently launched, and was failing miserably for unknown reasons. It was not your typical human rights field assignment—but it is not every country where women have to worry about getting attacked when they go to collect firewood. And in the wake of mass migration to the "safer" city and coastal areas, as well as severe overharvesting during the war, that wood-collecting walk took women an average of six hours a day. Tree planting—and fast—was a huge priority for the Sierra Leone government, given that the vast majority of the population depended on firewood for their daily nourishment.

My work involved long stretches of time in rural areas, where people generally ate just once a day given the extreme poverty that still permeated the country: rice with greens and some dried fish around 3:00 p.m. each afternoon. If variety is the spice of life, I wasn't getting much of it—and certainly I was getting a much lower calorie count than my US-raised body was accustomed to.

One afternoon I was passing through Bo Town, the capital of Bo Province in the southeastern part of Sierra Leone. I stopped by a streetside vendor for lunch—you guessed it, rice, greens, and dried fish for 500 leones a plate at the time, about the equivalent of 20 cents. I then went to a local market to stock up on the provisions I would need before making my next trip to the countryside. As badly as I felt about "sneaking" food into my room, I would buy Weetabix and other treats so that I could have at least two meals a day, a tremendous luxury in the village.

A shiny object on the cart of a woman street vendor caught my eye—a can of tuna! Sad to say, I was pretty excited about the idea of a tuna fish sandwich.

And then I picked up the can. Clearly stamped on it were these words:

World Food Programme: Not for Sale
Gift from the Government of Japan

I asked the woman how much she wanted for the can: 2,500 leones, she said, or just over $1. I pointed out the "Not for Sale" label, and asked where she had gotten the can. She just smiled back and indicated that, though she spoke at least three languages fluently, she couldn't read the can. She just wanted to know if I was going to buy it or not, and if not, I should let her go on with her business.

She was a convincing saleswoman; I bought the can. With the 2,500 leones I paid for it, this woman could buy five heaping plates full of her and her children's preferred meal. Talk about a rational economics lesson: Clearly, selling the tuna was her best possible use of it.

Luckily for her, I, essentially an aid worker with a US dollar–denominated stipend, had disposable income with which to purchase it from her, since clearly no one else locally was going to pay 2,500 leones for a can of tuna that was supposed to be a free gift. So thankfully the government of Japan had donated excess tuna to the World Food Programme, which transported it a little more than halfway around the world to feed starving people, so that a streetwise woman could realize she could eat about thirty-five times as many calories as it contained by selling it to a US aid worker.

Doing some very rough math on the equally rough ride back to the countryside, I calculated that the can of tuna generated at least one hundred times as much economic value for other people—including the Japanese fishermen, the government agents in Tokyo, and the World Food Programme office directors in Rome and Freetown—as it did for the supposed beneficiary. Presumably, the beneficiary of aid work is the one who receives the most benefit. It became crystal clear to me in that moment that if I pursued a career as an aid worker, the balance of my life's work was going to create much more value for those with power than for those without it.

STRUCTURAL LIMITATIONS TO AID

That story is simply a microcosm of the macro challenges of the aid system. Its irony has its origins in the way charitable resources are constructed to be a corrective mechanism and afterthought of our economic systems, in lieu of attempting to treat people right from the get-go. But the corrective mechanism isn't really corrective; the value of the goods and services and cash provided by government aid, charity, private philanthropy, etc., is simply a drop in the bucket of the global economy. It will never be able to provide enough resources to enough people, to liberate enough of their intelligence and energy and capacity, to enable them to successfully fight entrenched interests and rebuild an economy that will provide a better life for their children and their children's children.

Every year, US foundations give away approximately $46 billion. Yes, that's a lot of money—but not when one considers that some $196 trillion circulates in the global economy *every single day*. It's as if there were an oil spill covering 4,268 square miles of ocean, and you have been provided 1 square mile's worth of paper towels to try and mop it up. Good luck with that.[1]

Moreover, only 12 percent of this foundation giving goes to funding social justice endeavors.[2] That means that 88 percent of your 1 square mile's worth of paper towels will be off at the opera or the ballet, or busily writing its name on the side of a university building, and you'll now have exactly 230 square yards' worth of paper towels with which to mop up your 4,268 square miles of oil spill. Not that the arts and education aren't wonderful and important, but the vast majority of that giving is going to institutions that are already relatively wealthy, or predominately serve the wealthy, and that exist in the most affluent countries on the planet.

Finally, US foundations are legally required to give away a minimum of only 5 percent of their resources each year, with no requirement that their remaining resources, which by and large take the form of investments, have anything to do with their mission statements beyond generating revenue to give away more money.[3] Essentially, that means that foundations are allowed to have 95 percent of their financial activity operating in contradiction with their stated missions. It's an incredible tax and management loophole that very few sectors could get away with.

Just imagine, for a moment, that the president of an oil company spent 95 percent of his time on the golf course and

5 percent of his time in oil exploration. Or that you, despite being paid for a 9-to-5 desk job, only stuck your head in the office for 24 minutes a day. Wouldn't you both get fired?

Apparently, in the foundation world, you don't. However, slowly but surely, the world is waking up to this enormous loophole and attempting to expose and address it.

Back in 2007, the *Los Angeles Times*, my hometown paper, published a revelatory series of articles on the Gates Foundation vividly articulating the pitfalls of charity. The series created a visceral argument for aligning both financial and charitable investments with a clearly articulated set of values. The first article, "Dark Cloud Over Good Works of Gates Foundation," examined the dueling effects of the foundation's philanthropy and its investments in the Niger Delta. "The Gates Foundation," it said, "has poured $218 million into polio and measles immunization and research worldwide, including in the Niger Delta. At the same time that the foundation is funding inoculations to protect health, the *Times* found, it has invested $423 million in Eni, Royal Dutch Shell, Exxon Mobil Corp., Chevron Corp. and Total of France—the companies responsible for most of the flares blanketing the delta with pollution, beyond anything permitted in the United States or Europe."[4]

In business terms, it was as if the Gates Foundation had built a car company, and then sent two bulldozers to destroy each car that came off the assembly line. That's essentially what philanthropy is doing every day. It makes its money from investments in an extractive economy, then gives 5 percent of it away to try and fix the errors of the 95 percent.

Given its enormous endowment and influence, the Gates Foundation made an easy target, and over a decade later the foundation is now a very active impact investor. But at the time it was not doing anything that most other philanthropic institutions weren't also doing, and that many continue to do today. And, I dare say, it wasn't doing anything different from what we all do as everyday citizens who invest our money in financial institutions and make consumer choices blissfully unaware of their impact on people and the planet.

So what's our option instead? What is a do-gooder to do, if the charitable system keeps us locked in a David and Goliath battle?

As Carville advised Clinton. . . . It's the economy, stupid.[5]

two

ECONOMIC ACTIVISM
AND IMPACT INVESTMENT

THAT CAN OF TUNA HELPED ME RECOGNIZE THE LIMITS of aid and philanthropy, ultimately setting me on a new path toward impact investment. I started to think about how I could engage in the issues I cared about more effectively. Where was the real action happening? And what was my comparative advantage within the worldwide community of activists, in the context of a global economy dominated by US interests?

Like many of my college companions, I had been educated all my life to believe I could do anything, solve any problem. This sort of hubris has served me well in some ways—indeed, a feeling that I couldn't ever fail too hard is what has driven much of my entrepreneurship. But at times, I've had to give myself a reality check about the limits of individual effectiveness on two levels:

» The number-one rule social justice activists learn, especially those from relatively privileged backgrounds, is to take your lead from the affected community you seek to serve—and not just for the benefit of others, but for your own liberation as well. Your expertise may provide a critical contribution, but needs to be properly contextualized. Accept that you cannot determine someone else's priorities, and therefore can never act on your own to address a collective problem.

» Regardless of the mandate under which you work, there are limits to the efficacy of individual action within broken systems. Sometimes, you just have to change the system itself. To do that, you have to figure out where the heart of the problem really lies—and get right to it.

With these caveats in mind I recognized and internalized the futility, especially given my relative inexperience, of the efforts I was making—and that other young people from elite colleges were making alongside me—to "serve" in developing countries or even in US communities without having identified where we were most needed and could be most effective. We had fallen into the trap of focusing more on what was interesting to *us* than on what could be truly useful to others.

It also began to sink in that the pressing challenges I had hoped to address through development work—lack of food, clean water, housing, education, and sanitation—were largely being caused by global economic forces, and often by models, policies, and companies specifically created in the United States. If I wanted to help indigenous people in Ecuador who were suffering from the environmental and health impacts of

US oil companies operating in their region, getting on a plane to fight their local fight—as if I somehow knew how to do it better than they did—was unlikely to help. The most effective thing I could do as an American college student living in suburban Pennsylvania was to get US companies to clean up their act.

Holding oil companies accountable in Ecuador probably doesn't sound much easier to accomplish than getting food aid effectively into Sierra Leone. But as Americans, or citizens of any nation, we still have some vestiges of power over the politicians and corporations "born" on our soil. We just tend to give up our power a little too easily, rather than working to beat these forces at their own game.

A NATION OF UNKNOWING BILLIONAIRES

When activists take on a campaign, they often start out by building a "power analysis," mapping out who has power to change a situation, and then considering who or what can actually exercise influence over these centers of power. (Ideally, one would also work to alter these institutions such that power is not so closely held—but it's often a series of smaller policy victories that lead to overall structural change.)

Inevitably, a power map is riddled with money. Who profits from a certain status quo or harmful behavior, and what kind of change is needed to shift the circumstances such that it's no longer profitable to maintain it? What might help that party decide to make factors other than the classically defined bottom line a priority in their decision-making?

The assumption is typically that those who want to change an inequitable system have little access to resources—and that those of us who aren't white, college-educated, or from a wealthy background have even less access. We perceive institutions and the ultra-rich as the greatest holders of wealth, with a tiny percentage of individuals holding the rest—the so-called one percent and the ten percent. Because this reality is painful for those of us who are locked out of the financial elite, we may tend to avoid the subject of investment and its impact on economic systems. It just feels too far removed to take on effectively.

But when you consider who actually funds our wealthy institutions, and who they legally serve—and therefore who can wield influence over them—a different story emerges. As I discovered as a student at Swarthmore College, you may be a billionaire without knowing it.

Swarthmore, like many elite colleges, has an endowment of close to $2 billion.[1] As a nonprofit institution, it is legally obligated to invest its money in support of its educational mission and in service to its students. In this obligation it is no different from the California Public Employees' Retirement System (CalPERS), for example, which invests the pension funds of California teachers for their eventual benefit, and as such has control over the investment of nearly $300 billion, or the New York City Employee Retirement System (NYCERS), which is charged with safeguarding the pensions of the employees of New York City, to the tune of $47 billion.[2]

And like me, or the Oakland kindergarten teacher, or the Bronx sanitation worker, or a part-time minimum wage worker with a bank account at a large institution, just about everyone in the United States has some connection to an institution investing at least $1 billion. At a certain level we are all billionaires when it comes to influencing where money goes in the economy. The question becomes how we leverage these connections.

In 2007 I conducted a workshop on impact investment at the very first United States Social Forum (USSF), held that year in Atlanta. The USSF is a meeting of social activists that emerged from the World Social Forum (WSF). There was minimal publicity for the workshop, which was being held literally in a basement, and I had no idea who, if anyone, would attend. When I walked into the room, five white members of Resource Generation, a progressive organization that helps young wealthy donors effectively support social justice work, were already sitting in the front row, notebooks on their laps. "Great," I thought, "a nice small group with similar objectives. . . . We can have a real conversation here." Then, about ten minutes later, in walked a delegation of thirty or so black women in the bright purple shirts of the Service Employees International Union (SEIU). They had taken a bus from Texas to Atlanta for the conference. In our introductions, these women said that while they didn't expect to ever be millionaires, they knew that their pension fund was a source of power, and they were curious to know what the SEIU was up to and how they could think more proactively about their collective power as investors.

Each woman, if she was lucky, earned about $25 per hour as a nurse in Texas. But they were nevertheless connected to the $1 trillion in pension assets managed by the SEIU.[3] Their collective power was therefore far greater in some ways than that of the young, high-net-worth individuals represented by Resource Generation, and this power was a source of pride and conviction for them. The workshop opened up a conversation about power between two audiences that rarely connect. It was an affirmation that in a world in which the odds are stacked against historically disadvantaged communities in so many ways, there are access points to power that can be effectively leveraged precisely through what we usually see as the enemy: the world of finance.

When I was a college student, with both limited earning power and limited assets, my financial power was concentrated in the institution investing on my behalf. Swarthmore, like any other large institution, had its money invested just about every-where. Investments in a typical endowment or pension fund at a large institution like a university or union might include things like private prisons, oil and gas, military contractors, and harmful pesticides. These investments might be completely contrary to the values held by the people for whom the money is supposedly being invested, and they are often made without the supposed beneficiaries' knowledge or influence.

Once I learned about this, as a sort of run-of-the-mill activist who supported a variety of causes, I was no longer content to fight for fair-trade coffee in the cafeteria, or sweatshop-free shirts in the student store. Not that these issues weren't vitally important, but, budget-wise, Swarthmore's investment in cafeteria coffee was minuscule relative to the size of its endowment. To grossly oversimplify: Would you prefer to try to influence $10,000 per year of spending, or $1 billion of investments?

I joined the school's Committee on Socially Responsible Investment, which was charged with watching over and en-hancing the social and environmental profile of the school's endowment. During my first year as a member I proposed that we file a shareholder resolution with Lockheed Martin, an in-vestee of Swarthmore.[*] A shareholder resolution is a statement made in front of all of a company's shareholders that asks the

---

[*]Later, the student body would question whether Swarthmore, as a Quaker col-lege, should have been invested in a military manufacturer in the first place, but that issue was beyond the scope of this particular campaign.

company to take a specific action. It is considered to be the strongest action shareholders can take against a company short of giving up and selling the stock. All of a sudden, the company's dirty laundry is aired among the people they value most: their investors.

Lockheed Martin had a track record of quietly allowing poor treatment of queer people in the company. It was one of only a few Fortune 100 companies at the time that had not yet amended its antidiscrimination policy to include sexual orientation as a protected category. The gay rights organization among Lockheed employees, GLOBAL (Gay, Lesbian or Bisexual at Lockheed—in 2001 the full range of LGBTQ was not yet in vogue), had reported that gay employees around the country regularly received nasty notes that had been anonymously left on their desks; these employees would often try to get transferred to the California office, where discrimination was illegal by local law.

When our committee learned about this discrimination and decided to take action, we approached GLOBAL to let its members know about the shareholder activism route, and to ask if our interceding as investors would help their cause by encouraging corporate accountability not just to employees, but to shareholders as well. The group responded with an enthusiastic yes, and in the fall of 2001 we filed a shareholder resolution asking the company to add sexual orientation to its nondiscrimination policy.

Swarthmore was extremely supportive of what was essentially a student initiative. In April 2002, the vice president of finance at Swarthmore and I headed to the Lockheed Martin annual shareholder meeting in sunny San Diego. My father drove down from Los Angeles for the occasion.

We were quite the spectacle—Paul Aslanian, who as a gray-haired white man in roughly his late sixties fit the finance stereotype perfectly; and me, a nineteen-year-old college student, certainly the youngest person ever to present in front of the entire executive team and board of Lockheed Martin. While ageism and sexism have often proved challenging in my career, at this moment the united front of someone who represented a very traditional presentation of power, explicitly supporting the authoritative voice of a young woman, helped call attention to our cause and was something we ultimately used to our advantage.

Paul and I gave a passionate two-minute explanation of why a twenty-first-century company needed to treat all people equitably. We argued on a moral basis that it was simply the right thing to do, and we made an equally strong financial argument that insulting 10 percent of your potential workforce is undeniably a bad business decision.

The CEO responded that if Lockheed had to put sexual orientation into the nondiscrimination clause, they would soon "have to list brown-eyed and blue-eyed people. . . . When will it stop?"

Paul was able to get in one last rebuttal, and I'll never forget how proud I was of him in that moment for standing up for what he believed in. He looked the CEO in the eye and said, "I have two baby grandchildren, a blue-eyed girl and a brown-eyed girl. I am not so concerned that they will face discrimination based on their eye color, but I certainly fear they will face discrimination in the workplace, and notably, at your company, if one of them grows up to be gay." After that, we were led away by security guards in black suits. We joked that the heavy-handed security meant we must have been doing something right.

While the CEO's response at the meeting was quite negative, we could tell they heard us, and we knew they also must have noted all the great publicity we got everywhere from Fox News to the Associated Press in promulgating the first student-led shareholder resolution since the South African anti-apartheid initiatives of the 1970s and 1980s.[4]

That fall, Paul reached out to show me a front-page article in the *Washington Post*.[5] Lockheed had announced that it was adding sexual orientation to its nondiscrimination policy—it was even going to provide domestic partnership benefits for same-sex couples. The decision had come about through a combination of competitive pressure within the industry, our resolution, and years of organizing by Lockheed employees across the country, all of which had made it more and more challenging for Lockheed to resist change. About a year after I first broached the topic of filing a resolution, we were able to shout a rare phrase in the world of social change: "WE WON!"

I was absolutely thrilled—and quickly switched my focus to what is commonly referred to as the "saber-rattling" stage of corporate campaigns: leveraging a victory with one company to encourage others to adopt the same practice. We identified three other companies in the Swarthmore portfolio that also didn't have sexual orientation in their nondiscrimination policies—FedEx, Dover, and Masco. All three received roughly the same letter:

> *Dear Company X,*
>
> *You may have noticed that recently Lockheed Martin announced it would add sexual orientation to its non-discrimination clause and provide domestic partner benefits after receiving a shareholder resolution filed by*

*Swarthmore College. We have noticed that you also do not
have this policy in place, and that we equally own shares in
your company. Would you like to change this policy, or shall
we file another resolution and call the* Washington Post
back for a follow-up story? Just let us know your preference.

Sincerely,
*Rabble-rousing students plus supportive VP of Finance
on behalf of Swarthmore College, holding x shares of
your stock as part of a billion-dollar endowment*

The result: All three companies responded to us within a
month saying they would change their policy.[6]

I'm not saying all shareholder campaigns are this easy. In
this case, in just over a year, a tiny group of young people
successfully persuaded four Fortune 500 companies to change
their policies. In the process, I learned something incredibly
important about how powerful financial pressure can be. And
I was excited to share this knowledge with other young people
who were equally eager to make change.

Given all the news coverage about the resolution, students
excited about the idea of endowment activism started to write
from around the country, saying they wanted to do more. Five
of us joined together and launched the Responsible Endowments Coalition (REC), which initially brought together students from twenty-two campuses seeking to influence $56
billion in capital.[7]

In my three and a half years as the coalition's executive
director, we built a national movement on over one hundred
campuses holding over $150 billion. REC celebrated its tenth
anniversary in 2014, and is still going strong. Over the past
dozen years, the coalition has branched out far beyond its

initial shareholder advocacy program to support a variety of campaigns, from community investment to green loan funds to private prison divestment, and has become a key partner of progressive youth organizations like the Dream Defenders and 350.org. And slowly but surely, we got incorporated into the growing sector and practice called impact investment.

WHAT IS IMPACT INVESTMENT?

Impact investment is an attempt to align money with values. It is the practice of selecting for-profit investments in light of a growing awareness of the social and environmental outcomes of such investments. It's a simple but tremendously powerful concept that gets at the heart of the problem of segmenting the economy from charitable activity. Rather than playing with the $46 billion that constitutes the annual spending of philanthropy, we can leverage the $196 trillion that circulates in the global economy every day for social justice. Impact investment means that rather than trying to fight poverty with one arm tied behind our backs, dividing the world between business—which we perceive narrowly as a force that destroys people and the planet—and philanthropy—the leftover crumbs of the conventional economy designed to save us—we can come out swinging as hard as we can, bringing an entire society's resources to bear, and rebuild an economy that is sustainable, generative, and just.

In practice, it means that rather than putting money into fossil fuel investments, we can choose to finance renewable energy and projects that support the idea of a just transition away from a fossil fuel economy. It means that rather than putting money into a global bank that may engage in predatory practices, we can elect to keep our savings in a community-based institution that supports small business and low-income housing. And it means we can hold institutions accountable—whether they are pension funds, banks, or foundations—when by self-definition, charter, bylaws, or mission statement they are supposed to invest for the express benefit of their constituents.

The term *impact investing* itself was coined and popularized by the Rockefeller Foundation, which worked tirelessly to educate both philanthropists and investors about the potential of this new field.[8] While shareholder activism, screened funds, and other tools to seek impact within public equities had existed for decades, the framing of impact investment as a complete approach to portfolio management that could be scaled across the economy was new and ambitious when the Rockefeller Foundation first began its efforts in 2007.[9]

The origins of impact investment can be traced back even further, to the investment policies of the Quaker community, starting with their refusal to invest in the slave trade in 1758.[10] Going against the grain in an increasingly capitalist society in which decisions were made solely on the basis of financial return, the Quakers began to link their financial decisions to their values, additionally refusing to support "social ills" like alcohol, tobacco, and firearms. This point of view was taken up by several other religious denominations, including Methodists and some Catholic groups, but in general the practice was limited to a religious minority, and never embraced as a broader societal principle.

Over the past decade, however, major corporations and financial institutions have begun to reengage with social and environmental questions as they reckon with the reality that they cannot keep doing business as usual in a world that may disappear—a world in which the gap is widening between a very tiny wealthy elite and everybody else, and in which technological innovations have been insufficient to ensure the long-term health of the planet. Although different communities have varying interpretations of the reasons for these tectonic social, economic, and environmental shifts, and propose very different philosophical, political, and practical solutions to them, we are nevertheless at a historic moment in which an unusually high number of diverse constituents are deeply concerned with the question of how we will transform the global economy. Impact investment takes advantage of this moment and energy to scale new solutions.

A NOTE FOR SKEPTICS (AND SUPPORTERS)

There are many great reasons for both investors and activists to be skeptical of impact investment. Ironically, many of the people who reject the concept outright, before even exploring its potential, tend to do so for exactly opposite reasons: they think that impact investment is flawed either because it doesn't make enough money, or because it seeks to make money at all.

Investors worry that impact investments are simply not good investments—that they won't generate the value or return needed to fund critical activities, and from that perspective, that they will fail their intended beneficiaries. A retirement fund, for instance, is not much good to people if it doesn't grow in value.

Activists worry that investment as a strategy cannot escape its history as an instrument of an economic system that has tended to concentrate power in the hands of a privileged few, who have then exploited the powerless and neglected the consequences to human society and the planet. They may feel that investments, even when they are socially oriented, are still structurally flawed, as they perpetuate an extractive system that uses money to make money, whether or not it creates value for others in the process.

Advocates of impact investment should take both of these concerns seriously. Hence, before continuing a narrative that largely assumes that impact investment has great potential as a tool for transformative social change, I want to thoroughly address these common critiques.

CAN IMPACT INVESTMENTS MAKE MONEY?

Investors often reject impact investment because they assume it doesn't make money as efficiently as traditional investing. Investment's job is to make money; making change is charity's job. Therefore, they argue, investments should make as much money as possible, allowing charity to then give away as much as possible. Mixing the two makes both less efficient, as they serve very different functions. As Marc Andreessen of the venture capital firm Andreessen Horowitz famously said of impact investment, "It's like a houseboat. It's not a great house and not a great boat."[11]

This argument assumes that markets are the most efficient way to distribute resources, and that therefore we should let them work their magic to the fullest—then clean up their mistakes with philanthropy (and, ideally, some degree of government policy and regulation on the front end). That in itself is an idea to question. But let's first take seriously the notion that some institutions need to make money to serve their constituencies—and may even be legally obligated to show they have made their best efforts to do so. To those who doubt that impact investment can make money as well as the traditional financial system, I would ask you to think like a good investor and check out the relative track records of traditional versus impact investments.

From a macro perspective, it's impossible to ignore that while the financial system has enabled pockets of society to make short-term wealth, endless growth that is based on the unlimited use of natural resources and endlessly cheap labor is simply unsustainable. That was a great strategy for a century or two, but even the most conservative institutions acknowledge that its time has passed.

Mike Musuraca, who served as a designated trustee of the New York City Employee Retirement System for over a decade, used to always say that regardless of any moral stance, his organization didn't have the luxury of ignoring the social and environmental outcomes of the financial system. With over $40 billion in assets, NYCERS essentially owned the whole market, and thus if a particular corporation "externalized" its social or environmental costs, NYCERS would just take on this weight somewhere else in the portfolio.[12]

If even the largest asset-owners on the planet—NYCERS, CalPERS, etc.—feel that the current system is not working in their favor, then something is deeply wrong. If you simply deepen your expertise in financial management without considering the social and environmental impact of investments, your services will be of limited use to savvy asset owners.

From a micro perspective, even if you excluded externalities, and just focused on financial track records, study after study has shown that impact investments have been able to outperform the market with lower levels of volatility. This has been shown across asset classes and through portfolio-based approaches that will be highlighted throughout this book.[13]

To take an example from one asset class to start, some segments of the investment industry, such as venture capital, have talked a big talk while producing limited returns. In 2006, *Harvard Business Review* concluded that "VC funds haven't significantly outperformed the public markets since the late 1990s, and *since 1997 less cash has been returned to VC investors than they have invested*. A tiny group of top-performing firms do generate great 'venture rates of return': at least twice the capital invested, net of fees. We don't know definitively which firms are in that group, because performance data are not generally available and are not consistently reported. *The average fund, however, breaks even or loses money*" (emphasis mine).[14]

The Ewing Marion Kauffman Foundation, the premier research institution on entrepreneurship, concluded, somewhat more optimistically, that "the average VC fund fails to return investor capital after fees."[15]

If that's market rate for venture-style investments, then meeting or beating market rate should not be too substantial of a challenge. Whether or not the sole objective of investment should be to make as much money as possible is something worth grappling with, but if your instinct is to dismiss impact investing based on the rate of return, this may not be your best argument.

I would also counter Marc Andreessen's houseboat comment with apocryphal wisdom from Warren Buffett. During a business school lecture, a student asked Buffett whether, if you wanted to have positive social impact, it made sense to make a bunch of money as quickly as possible first, and give it away later. Buffett is said to have replied: "Isn't that a little like saving up sex for your old age?"[16]

I have spoken to so many financial advisors over the course of my career who are invigorated by the idea that they could have a meaningful career today, not just post-retirement. It's no accident that at Harvard Business School, the Social Enterprise Club has become one of the largest clubs on campus, with its annual event attracting more than 1,500 participants; or that more than 100,000 students globally have joined Net Impact, the association for business school students who seek to have impactful careers.[17] Whether these people will stop short at "doing well by doing good," rather than aiming for transformative change, is a major question. The challenge for aspiring impact investors and entrepreneurs is not just whether they will have an impactful career, but whether they will be able to truly maximize their potential for impact.

SHOULD IMPACT INVESTMENTS MAKE MONEY?

People with a deep commitment to social justice often reject the idea of impact investing because it makes money at all. Given that investment has historically been used to concentrate wealth, and the resultingly high concentration of wealth in today's society, many feel that it's impossible, by definition, for any structure that enables the wealthy to amass more wealth, even if it serves a social purpose along the way, to be transformational.

Before we even get to the question of impact investment, let's talk for a moment about what an investment actually is. An investment, at its most basic level, is designed to take resources and turn them into more resources.

It's connected to the very ancient practice of commerce—the exchange of goods and services that presumably makes everyone in the interaction feel that their time and resources have been fairly valued and traded. Exchange is not a bad thing, particularly given how useful specialization can be in a society. I might enjoy gardening and could feed myself well enough, but when the revolution comes, I sincerely hope I don't have to make my own shoes. I don't know a society where trade and investment are not central concepts, and whether it's collecting seeds to plant more fruit, or building a boat with which to fish for the next decade, using resources one day to try and garner more resources the next feels like a fundamental building block of human striving and indeed thriving. Even subsistence farmers in rural areas need to produce more than they themselves will eat if they want to be able to sell their surplus in order to pay for a child's education, purchase clothes or medicine, or simply survive a season of crop failure. Take the exploitation out of investment, and you can have something quite useful.

However, throughout history and still today, investment has rightfully earned its reputation as a major contributor to global inequality. We can, and should, debate the merits of who has money, who doesn't have money, and how investment structures have been among the Western world's most effective innovations in cementing inequities with respect to race, gender, and class. Let's not forget, for instance, that the foundations of modern trade finance were designed to serve slavery.[18] I will assume my readers are aligned with the idea that structural inequity—not just economic but social, political, and cultural—is not only morally deplorable, but arguably our largest barrier to progress as a species, and that it no longer deserves to be the objective of finance.

So if investment has the potential to be a useful instrument, but has been largely hijacked over the past five hundred years as a tool for the concentration of wealth, then is impact investment a way to bring finance back to its roots in human exchange and (reasonable) resource accumulation, or is it just another way of putting window-dressing on the same project of global theft? Is it possible to decouple investment from the general project of reinforcing inequality?

I would argue that investment, and commerce generally, is a neutral tool, but that given its historical legacy it needs *exceptional* guidance to succeed in not propagating injustice. Just as the absence of effective government does not lead most of us to endorse anarchy, the economy's failures should lead us to seek more effective practices, not to eliminate the idea of investment.

We would have trouble existing as a society without some form of collective economy, one that invests in itself to grow. Using communal resources to create more resources is generally a good thing when managed responsibly. We see this play out in the diversity of what investment has become, and the variety of circumstances in which it occurs. It happens in pension funds that enable teachers, firefighters, public servants, and other middle-income individuals to retire at a reasonable age. When people fear the erosion of the Social Security system (and safety net), they know that its solvency rests on investments. It happens in the context of savings co-ops and credit unions that help rural farmers co-enable survival by making investments in each other, and sharing the proceeds of these investments such that no one is exploited. I have seen many activists support these sorts of mutual financial support systems, just without calling them "investments" or recognizing them as simply a more just implementation of this ancient tool. It also happens with wealthy individuals and institutions who make choices about how their investment proceeds are used. And it happens with foundations, who can choose to recycle investment earnings into more philanthropic contributions or social investments.

In this light, we can then refine our questions. It's not just whether investments are good or bad, but what resources are being created through investments, and are they are good for people and the planet? Who is making money from an investment, and what are they choosing to do with it?

I invite people to deeply consider both of these questions, and even to challenge impact investors with them. We must return to these questions each and every time an impact investment is made, and, in my view, structure our investments to try, first and foremost, to create value for those who have been historically locked out of access to resources. Second, we must work to recycle these resources to serve more and more communities.

It is true that some people are going to make more wealth in this process—and "how much is enough" is a fundamental societal question worth addressing. Whether the system of wealth creation is sufficiently accessible to all people is another critical issue for consideration.

But although it is essential that we closely examine who benefits from an investment, the fact that investments make money is not a valid argument for avoiding engaging in impact investment. You're not necessarily evil if you make money from an investment. And, equally, you're not necessarily virtuous if you give money away. But you do have a lot of choices to make if you want to jump into impact investment and empower, rather than exploit, people in the process.

Both of these perspectives tie into the question of how we define "market rate" for the field. As they talk among themselves, impact investors tend to divide the universe of investments into two categories: "market rate" and "below market rate." This distinction of course begs the question: What is market rate? And what does it have to do with social investments?

Typically, market rate is defined as the typical return an investor will receive for an asset class in any given sector or geographic region. The underlying investments that help determine the benchmark may include, once again, investments in truly despicable things—prisons, factories using sweatshop labor, land deals displacing small farmers, and so on. Is this really what we want as our standard of comparison? Or should we start by thinking about what would actually be a *reasonable return* that would create long-term benefit for all? This redefinition of what constitutes a successful return on a social investment might be a radical one, but if we actually want to create a more just society, we might have to change the rules of the game.

In this new game, the good news is we still get to have profit. The idea is that *all* parties involved in an interaction should make a return that is honest, transparent, and proportionate to their efforts.

FROM FIGHTER TO LOVER

As a newly committed economic activist at the Responsible Endowments Coalition, I became more and more excited by the promise of this new field called impact investment. So when the time came for me to move on from REC, I took on the role of founding CEO at Toniic, a social enterprise that has grown to support more than three hundred impact investors looking to dedicate over $4.5 billion to impact investing.

Toniic started out focusing on early-stage deals, and during my three and a half years as CEO, I reviewed over five hundred deals and helped investors lead investments into thirty-three of them. We quickly expanded into full portfolio approach work, looking at impact investment across all asset classes. In general, these years provided me with a fantastic introduction to the world of impact investment and made me ever more convinced of its potential.

When I transitioned from REC to Toniic, part of the reason for my transition was that while I was still invigorated by the idea of leveraging investment dollars for impact, I was tired of fighting all the time. As much progress as the coalition had made in getting corporations to change their practices, we had not fundamentally altered their priorities in pursuing profit first and foremost. For the majority of companies, positive social and environmental outcomes were still tangential to their primary focus; nice, if they didn't inhibit profit-making, but not a primary purpose. I wanted to be not just a fighter, but a lover—someone who wasn't just targeting what was wrong with the world, but who was also participating in building viable alternatives to our current economic system. Like many activists, I had spent so much time getting my heart broken by what was wrong in the world that my ability to envision a brighter future had itself dimmed.

This desire to become more solutions-focused was con-nected to the evolution of my thinking about "poverty"—

which I began to understand as a crisis of autonomy, both individual and collective—and what was required to solve it. I thoroughly internalized the idea that poverty is not about whether or not you have a TV, or in general meet some specific set of standards set by an outside authority, but is something deeply personal. It's about whether or not you have *choice*: Do you get to make fundamental decisions about how to live your life? Do you have cultural, political, social, and economic autonomy? Are your basic needs fulfilled in a way to even enable you to take a breath and consider other elements of life beyond daily survival?

Time after time I felt like economic autonomy was the essential factor that allowed other forms of community autonomy to be actualized. When you have your own resources, you are less subject to someone else telling you how to live, what religion you have to practice, when and how much to work, and so on. Having your own resources also allows you the mental space to be creative and engaged. Hence, rather than fighting poverty, my new goal was to try to enhance community autonomy—and specifically, economic autonomy—both domestically and globally.

So I set out with my new, lofty goal, unsure of how to pursue it. As the history of colonialism teaches us, for a global power suddenly to decree that the community it's been robbing blind for centuries is now autonomous can mean setting that community up for failure. So my specific task became: *How does one replace historically stolen resources within communities in a way that enhances autonomy?*

Investment seemed like one effective way to pursue this goal. Rather than keeping communities dependent on donations, the power of investment is that it aligns the community and investor around a common goal: sustainability and long-term self-sufficiency.

As a micro-level explanation of the power of impact investment as a tool for community autonomy, consider two (over-simplified) cases of how one could approach an agricultural project in Ghana.

In Model 1, a local nonprofit gives free tractors to an agricultural community in rural Ghana. To receive the annual funds needed to maintain the tractors and purchase other inputs, such as seeds, the organization must petition someone in the donor's office in New York, proposing what they think they need and negotiating with the donor, who might disagree and propose an alternative according to what they think is best, or set conditions on their donation. Money is deployed based on the judgment of the program officer and the restricted universe in which they must operate—until the president of the foundation decides the new area of need is India. The project in Ghana is abandoned, and the tractors fall into disrepair.

In Model 2, the investor and the community in Ghana work together to figure out the appropriate business model for farmers. How much will tractors increase their productivity, and thus how profitable can they be? How much do the farmers need to make to be able to afford maintenance and inputs over time? Tractors are purchased through a loan, and repayment of the loan requires strong accounting practices to be adopted. This helps the farmers learn how to better manage their cash flow, which proves useful not just for the loan repayment, but also for farming households to be prepared for major expenses, such as school fees. After five years, the loan is paid off and the farmers have enough income to buy their own inputs. The investor can go off to fund another community—or could let those original dollars be set up as a long-term loan fund under community control. At that point, the investor won't have a say over the farmers' decisions unless specifically invited to play a role—and ideally by that point as well, the investor's expertise will have proven itself to be a desirable input rather than an imposed one. Most importantly, some of those historically stolen resources will have been replenished in the form of community wealth.

It would be incorrect to say that power dynamics are completely absent from Model 2—we cannot deny the history and reality of who has resources nowadays in the first place. It would also be incorrect to say that Model 1 has no positive impact at all in the short term. The critical distinction in Model 2 is the *long-term, systemic outcome*: the transition of decision-making, skills, and assets from the hands of a few to the hands of many, and the way that new dynamic sets up a community or a nation for a much more balanced society.

So this is where my story diverges a bit from the classic narrative of "disgruntled aid worker decides that market solutions are a superior form of development," an ideological framework often reiterated in the impact investment world. I had no interest in replicating American-style markets across the world (or even encouraging their continuation within the United States, for that matter). Replicating markets that are extractive and abusive by nature in other environments will only deepen the imbalances of power and resources that have become a feature—or shall we say, an "unavoidable externality"—of the American system.

What I *did* see in impact investment was the potential to replenish resources in a way that builds community power and autonomy, to create new business models that prioritize well-being and "gross national happiness" (as they say in Bhutan), and to leverage profits for community asset creation rather than wealth extraction. How to get from vision to actual practice, however—that is where the challenge begins.

three

THE LIMITS OF IMPACT INVESTMENT

JUST AS I STARTED TO SEE GREAT POTENTIAL IN IMPACT investment as a tool for economic transformation and empowerment, it dawned on me that this was not yet a central objective for the field. And the more I became involved with impact investment, the clearer it seemed to me that the industry was essentially re-creating the financial world as it was, with a slight social twist. "Doing well by doing good" is a start, but we needed to be building something new, the *primary* goal of which would be to solve societal problems through sustainable, profitable models. There was lots of new investment activity, across all sorts of asset classes, geographies, and sectors, but little evidence of systemic change. Function was following form—and something was getting lost in the process.

Struggling to reconcile these contradictions led me to my next steps: working to establish a framework for impact investment that would truly enhance community autonomy, and by extension, fight poverty in all its forms. I started to recognize the industry trends that were limiting impact investment's potential for transformative change, many of which continue to manifest to this day. These are general trends and don't apply in every case—but I have seen them time and time again over the past decade, and fear they will become endemic through inertia unless collectively acknowledged and addressed.

Investors who become involved in impact are by and large well-intentioned and serious about wanting to help poor communities and strengthen the planet's ecosystems, while continuing as responsible professionals to make profits for themselves, their firms, or their clients. But we inherit a long history of imbalanced relationships around money, and thus are sometimes unconscious that we share a set of assumptions and standard operating procedures that work to blunt the force of impact and inhibit genuine economic transformation. Although the field of impact investment has tremendous potential, we need to proceed with caution, particularly in the following eight areas.

1. Investors and Entrepreneurs Profit at the Expense of Communities

The goal of impact investment for many is to have a social impact while still being able to earn the same kind of return on investment that conventional markets have provided. But if impact investment is going to address systemic inequities, we need to think about who owns and controls social enterprises—and who, in turn, is benefiting from them. *If the ownership of social enterprises remains limited to the privileged*, then it is difficult to imagine how impact investments can ultimately maximize benefit to communities, or facilitate any sort of significant resource transfer from the Global North to the Global South (or generally within any nation, from rich to poor).

If ownership structures are not addressed, then by definition these investments must be extracting value, and thus repeating the cycle of exploitation that we have seen under so many different names over the decades. The reiteration of status quo resource inequity is particularly apparent in the context of projects whose stakeholders see poor communities solely as consumers rather than as participants in all aspects of the economic cycle. There is an implicit, yet often unacknowledged, tension in impact investment between how much producers are paid, how much consumers pay for products, and how much entrepreneurs and investors can make or expect to make over time.

Profitability, of course, is essential for the long-term sustainability of any enterprise. Profit is also critical for social enterprises, but it is far less transformative when ownership, and hence the right to partake in profit, is limited to a global elite, as opposed to being shared more broadly. Impact investors should recognize this liability and structure deals that ensure a more equitable sharing of profits that accompanies solutions that are structured for long-term impact.

2. Impact Is Being Defined by Investors and Entrepreneurs Instead of Beneficiaries

Impact investment has evolved as a "top-down" industry, with investors setting the criteria for impact and returns, and the consequences filtering down from fund managers to social entrepreneurs to communities. This structure essentially makes

it impossible for communities to set the agenda according to
their own needs. Well-meaning entrepreneurs tend to limit
community involvement to product research, such as holding
focus groups, rather than creating infrastructure for long-term
engagement and community leadership development based
on community priorities. And even if they seek to establish a
different and deeper relationship with a community—which
they are rarely provided with the time or resources to do—
they are likely to struggle to find funding sources willing to
support the process.

   I typically attend two or three impact investment conferences annually—including SOCAP, the Social Capital Markets
Conference, the largest gathering on social enterprise in the
United States—as well as a few "social movement" conferences, such as the World Social Forum—the world's largest
gathering of grassroots groups. Over the years I have often
had to pay out of my own pocket to attend the social justice
conferences, since they were not always seen as "business es-
sentials," but I felt that maintaining some line of connection
and accountability to social movements was crucial to our investment work. It broke my heart that time after time, I would
be the only investor there; and perhaps because of the history
of disconnection between the two groups, activists would at
times even ask me with some hostility what I was doing there.

   It was remarkable how rarely the conversations at impact
investment conferences and social justice conferences inter-
sected. The investors talked about things like "FinTech," or
financial technology, and "health-care IT," terms hard to de-
cipher for anyone who was not part of the Silicon Valley eco-
system. Social justice leaders talked about "land grabs" and
"environmental racism," phrases perhaps equally incompre-

hensible to the average investor. If investors are not intimately aware of and connected to the priorities of social movements, how can they effectively set their own priorities?

Some investors are doing an exemplary job of connecting with communities, and proving it is possible to develop scalable impact models in response to community needs. For instance, the John D. and Catherine T. MacArthur Foundation has been making donations to address both US immigration policy and global migration since 2012, implementing strategies designed to make "fundamental improvements in migration policies and practices."[1] Its grantee partners did a lot of the groundwork for President Barack Obama's 2014 announcement on immigration, which expanded Deferred Action for Childhood Arrivals (DACA) and created the Deferred Action for Parents of Americans (DAPA) program, opening the doors for an additional 4 million people already in the United States to receive legal work status and a pathway to citizenship—or what Obama himself described as the opportunity to "come out of the shadows."

This opportunity was exciting for many immigrant families, but it didn't come cheap—it required a $465 application fee per person and often a consultation with a lawyer to make sure everything was properly handled. Hence the average applicant needed at least $1,000 to be able to participate—a sum out of the reach of many struggling immigrants.

Grassroots grantees floated this conundrum up to members of an alliance called the Grantmakers Concerned with Immigrant Refugees (GCIR), and the GCIR director looked to the MacArthur Foundation for help. Foundation leadership realized that this was a great opportunity for impact capital to support a product that addressed a community's need in timely fashion. Given the fact that legalized work status was proven to lead to substantial increases in income for migrant workers, it made sense that a loan could be structured such that it wouldn't be overly burdensome and could ultimately enable participants to build wealth.

The MacArthur Foundation then approached Self-Help Federal Credit Union, which had deep roots working in Latinx communities across the country. Self-Help had already been developing such a product as part of its suite of financial services for low-income immigrants. MacArthur offered to bring together investors to support Self-Help in expanding its DACA/DAPA loan product. Loans would be coupled with the opportunity to open a bank account at Self-Help, so that low-income clients could develop a financial relationship with a community-based financial institution focused on fulfilling their needs, rather than going instead to payday lenders designed to extract value from low-income communities. MacArthur knew the loan to Self-Help needed to be a long-term one—but, aware that some other investors wouldn't be able to hold out that long, it offered to serve as a backstop and, if necessary, "cash out" those investors before the ten-year term of the loan was over.

Unfortunately, the future of DACA/DAPA became uncertain even during the Obama administration, and tragically, by the time this book is in your hands, these programs may no longer even exist. In short, the partners had to put this idea on ice. Still, I love this story, because it highlights three different practices that more investors should emulate:

» MacArthur responded to a very current, broad, and tangible need articulated by grassroots partners via a funder affinity group that positioned itself to do the deep listening, rather than setting its own priorities and then seeking out investable institutions.

» MacArthur not only leveraged the opportunity to solve a short-term issue (how to expand the DACA/DAPA loan product), but also went a step further to try and address the longer-term *systemic* issue of the lack of positive banking relationships accessible to immigrant communities.

» MacArthur set investment terms that made sense for its partner, Self-Help Federal Credit Union, such that it could serve its low-income clients, and then figured out on its own how to make it work for investors, rather than putting this burden on the institution.

It's this sort of bottom-up product design that can help shape the impact investment industry so that it is truly responsive to community needs, in dynamic relationship with the changing political and financial landscape that communities face.

3. Impact Investment Is Taking the "Easy Wins"—Celebrating Incremental Change Rather Than Restructuring Economic Systems

The "easy win" phenomenon is apparent in practically every sector of impact investment, from the pricing of microfinance products to job creation. In essence, it is a consequence of how impact is defined overall.

Some of the large financial institutions moving into impact investing have made public statements defining impact as simply any investment made in a developing country—or, as it is often labeled in the Global North, in an "emerging domestic market"—the logic being that any investment will at the very least create jobs for poor people. But the many communities that have suffered from natural resource extraction, displacement, and poor labor conditions know that the price of some jobs is just too high—and that the typical low-paying job offered only serves to cement cycles of poverty.

And yet, a large percentage of impact investments have gone to what are commonly referred to as SMEs (small and medium enterprises) or SGBs (small and growing businesses). Few standards regarding what companies produce and how they treat their workers or the environment guide these investment decisions, and the companies effectively get subsidized capital from well-meaning governments, foundations, and private investors to conduct business as usual.

This theme plays out in many different ways domestically and globally. One impact fund, for example, was founded on the premise of supporting job creation in the United States. But when I spoke with one of the fund's managers and asked them for a success story, they spoke about a company they'd invested in that had created hundreds of jobs for low-income workers in a service industry. I said, "That's great. Can you share a bit about the quality of those jobs?" Their founding partner's response: "Well, most of them are Mexicans, so we started buying them tickets to soccer games. Since we started doing that, Workers' Comp claims fell from $2 million to $1.2 million, as they sue us less when they quit."

Another US-based impact fund supporting SMEs in developing countries invested in a clothing import business bringing goods from Asia to South Africa, calling it an "impact investment" because it served all market segments, including poor consumers. Some South Africans from the social sector who learned about this investment were livid. In a popular social enterprise publication, they wrote a critique referencing the "serious potential negative impacts that could result from bringing more cheap clothes made in Asia to the South African market."[2] The article essentially said, "If your definition of impact is displacing our local jobs and industry that we've worked so hard to build, we'd prefer you stay at home."

Other projects may have some clearly positive impact, but while they create something that is better than the next available alternative, they stop short of what would perhaps be a more equitable and systemic change.

To provide a very simple example, take the case of solar home systems, which have swept the globe as an important alternative to kerosene. These systems typically provide light and a small amount of electricity for activities like phone charging at a price a penny cheaper than kerosene, but with huge health benefits and a much better quality of light. People were happy to pay for them given that they were so much better than the alternative. And that meant the donors and investors were happy with the impact being achieved.

At the end of the day, however, these solar home systems still provide energy at roughly $5 per kilowatt-hour, compared to the roughly 12.2 cents per kilowatt-hour that a consumer in the Global North pays for solar energy (which, given advances in technology, is thankfully about comparable to non-renewables, which clock in at 12 cents per kilowatt-hour, on average).[3] Sure, it is still better than kerosene. But no one was asking the essential questions: Was this product actually priced fairly, and was it providing a long-term solution? Or was it just slightly less unfair than the alternative? Did it change the overall equation for energy-impoverished users? It's critical at this stage in impact investment's development for us to always stop and ask whether this intervention is not only better, but actually transformative to the people it intends to serve.

4. There Is a Major "Capital Gap" for Community-Run Projects

Although many investment projects are carried out in the Global South, they are generally run by those with greater access both to education and to the outside world. These entrepreneurs and their investors are the ones who will receive the $183 billion to $667 billion in profit that J. P. Morgan projects will be actualized over the next decade.[4] It is, at this point, exceptionally rare, if not impossible, for communities, organizations, or individuals from the Global South to receive access to funds if they do not speak English and lack advanced degrees. In the Global North, individuals without a sterling investment track record also rarely get access. The current industry structure limits communities to serving as the resource base via employment, or as the consumer base for specific products, such as stoves or financial services. As is the case when it comes to aid, communities are still largely recipients rather than protagonists.

Once again, this phenomenon is connected to the top-down nature of the industry. The size of checks and terms of deals are dependent on what the investment industry structures as feasible, rather than in response to community needs. More community-minded projects often get caught in the trap of appearing to be too small or too low-yielding to be bothered with. For example, a community grocery store in West Oakland, California, without plans for national expansion may not seem worth the time to underwrite, even though there is sufficient local market for it to operate profitably and its potential benefit for the community is substantial. On the other hand, some projects are deemed too big and complex to be entrusted to community members—as in the case of Grupo Yansa, an enterprise promoting utility-scale, community-owned wind energy, which we'll explore in more depth in Chapter 6. It may be that in the short term these questions will be solved through philanthropy, and indeed, the world needs more of it as part of the solution—but in the long run, if we want to really activate capital for social change, we will need an industry that is a lot more accessible to a broader community.

5. Capacity Building and Start-Up Capital Is Lacking for the 99 Percent

Capacity-building programs for social entrepreneurs to receive business training and access to funding are plentiful, but similarly limited to few, and typically only those who have already attained a high level of formal education can participate. For others who would like to get involved in social entrepreneurship, particularly to build their own, community-based businesses, the barriers to entry can be substantial.

Some readers may recall a 2007 book called *The Revolution Will Not Be Funded: The Non-Profit Industrial Complex.*[5] Its condemnation of the philanthropy industry was powerful, and it inspired many activists—including close friends of mine who were once skeptical of my work—to seek out alternative forms of revenue generation for their movement organizations and nonprofits.

This was personally very gratifying, but I quickly realized that I had incredibly little to offer. There were no training courses I could name at the time that cost less than $2,000, or didn't require you to already have an enterprise in place, and most of the enterprises I knew had gotten their start-up capital either through business plan competitions—that required competitors to be business school students—or from that unique category in angel investing referred to as "friends and family."

I have been friends with a young woman from Los Angeles for close to two decades. She is from a working-class immigrant family, and we connected when I volunteered throughout the late 1990s at a social service agency called Para Los Niños, which serves the largely Latinx downtown community. A few years ago I was going on a site visit to a social enterprise and invited her to join me. Given the fact that she'd known me since I was in high school, when she was in third grade, I was proud to get to share some of my work life with her.

On the site visit I asked the entrepreneur how she got her start-up capital, and she said, "Well, our first $500k came from friends and family."

My friend and I locked eyes, and I could see her wheels turning: "$500,000 . . . from *friends and family*?"

I am fairly confident that if my young friend wanted to start her own social business, and tried to pass the hat in her neighborhood, she would be lucky to get $500.

It's not that the woman who successfully raised $500k from friends and family wasn't capable and talented (I can affirm that she is!)—and surely she had to prove that to her friends and family before they would be willing to invest. I have certainly relied on friends and family in the past to support my efforts, particularly philanthropically. The issue is that she and I are very lucky to have access to networks that have the *ability* to support us. The friends and families of other would-be entrepreneurs certainly love them no less. The idea that entrepreneurs should be given so few pathways to start their businesses beyond relying on a "family and friends round" is ridiculous and even sometimes downright insulting; it reinforces the classist nature of entrepreneurship. Entrepreneurship is a birthright for some, and an incredible struggle for others. The lack of investment opportunities for those who do not have outside support to get to a proof of concept severely limits global entrepreneurship—and, as Mitch and Freada Kapor, prolific early-stage impact investors, often note, "genius is evenly distributed by zip code; opportunity is not."[6]

6. Impact Investors Have a Long Way to Go in Addressing Race and Gender Dynamics Within the Industry

In Silicon Valley, it is often assumed that good ideas always win the day—that race and gender have nothing to do with investment. Class privilege, such as access to "friends and family," may make a difference, but race and gender should not. That may be conceptually true, but it is a functional myth, and not just in the tech industry. Unless impact investment creates significantly different structures to prevent us from replicating the same sort of systems as those in conventional investing, we will continue to hide our heads under the false blanket of race blindness, and hence fall short of both our potential impact and our financial goals.

For such a numbers-oriented industry, venture capital is incredibly tone-deaf with respect to its own stats. Demographic data paints a very clear picture of what's actually happening. Table 1 shows the percentage of members of different groups

TABLE 1: Demographics of Venture Capital in Silicon Valley

Demographics	White	Latino	Black	Asian	Women	Men
US Demographics (2014 Census Data)	62%	17%	13%	5%	49%	51%
Silicon Valley Firm Demographics (Senior Investment Team)	78%	1%	1%	20%	8%	92%
Silicon Valley Deal Demographics	78%	1%	1%	20%	2%	98%

involved in venture capital deals in Silicon Valley compared to the demographics of Silicon Valley firm management and the overall US population. Essentially, it shows how venture capital demographics follow the demographics of the tech industry in the region: deals are overwhelmingly made by white males, with Asian men coming in at a distant second place.

This imbalance in venture capital is somewhat understandable, given the fact that most venture capitalists live in communities that reflect their own demographic categories, which makes it harder to recognize one's own blind spots. But if we want to paint the industry as a race-blind, gender-blind utopia, we are being willfully blind to reality.[7]

I am sorry to say that I do not have commensurate statistics for the impact investment industry—but can provide ample anecdotal data about the lack of acknowledgment that we cannot build a successful industry in a majority-minority world if we do not pay attention to the diversification of our talent pool. In short, it's not just that we are lacking diversity in our industry—we lack awareness that this is even a problem. Acknowledging this problem would require us to see the internalized racism that can lead us to make certain decisions about whom to hire or fund or engage with—decisions that may be made completely unconsciously given our cultural training. Here are just a couple of examples of how the tone-deafness of venture capital is being replicated in impact investing:

» My firm was once pitched by a fund investing in Africa and Latin America with a slide showing eight team members and the headline: "We have the perfect team to invest in Africa and Latin America." The team? Eight white men.

» One of our favorite funds, Cross Culture Ventures, is led by two black partners. Despite the partners having over ninety investments between them, and a sterling track record including hits like Spotify, Warby Parker, and Uber, they were having serious trouble fundraising. Later the feedback came, behind closed doors, that investors were concerned that their portfolio was going to be "too black." I'm happy to say the managers took this energy and decided to prove everyone wrong, and ultimately they successfully closed their first fund—but they got the message loud and clear that they wouldn't have had such difficulty if they had been white.

Some exemplary investors, such as Kapor Capital, Impact America, Cross Culture Ventures, and Bronze Investments, have made the acknowledgment of a majority-minority world explicit to their investment thesis, using tools like the Founders' Commitment, a list of ways entrepreneurs can be more thoughtful about diversity, to try and proactively address the need to expand the industry. Oddly, these funds are the exception rather than the rule. Should the concept that investors and entrepreneurs will be successful if they represent the people they aim to serve be so novel? My concern is not just about the lack of diversity in the industry, but about the lack of awareness of how urgent a priority this issue should be, that requires concrete action to be addressed beyond just a desire for change.

Gender dynamics in the industry are not much better. In this case, as a white woman, I can speak to this topic from personal experience. I confess that for many years I was a feminist the same way I'm Jewish—I knew it was a part of me, but I didn't actively identify or engage as such. Being an investor has really shifted that for me because of the challenges I have experienced on account of my gender. It's not just the fact that these challenges are annoying and uncomfortable—that I can ultimately tolerate, and generally get a good laugh at as well. I am mostly concerned that gender bias keeps us from doing our best work together in an industry that needs every possible person and perspective to make it effective. The statistics about the dearth of women working in the investment field are one thing. But it's the everyday behaviors of people in the industry toward women that are the most frustrating to me. If these could be addressed through some greater efforts at personal accountability, it would likely make the investment field a much more hospitable place for women.

Sexism has consistently, quietly lurked in the background of my professional encounters over the past fifteen years. Men have asked me if I'm the secretary—or whether they should talk to my boss—despite the "Executive Director" or "CEO" or "Managing Director" title clearly printed on my business card. To date I have never had a woman ask me these questions.

Similarly, despite my title and photo being both on my card and on our firm's website, I have spent years correcting "Dear Mr. Simon" emails. Is it that hard to imagine that the CEO of an investment organization might actually be a woman? Other times, the fact that I was a woman was apparently front and center for new connections who would set up business meetings under false pretenses—for example, once I showed up to a meeting to find an investor presenting me with flowers and refusing to talk about work, because he wanted to "get to know me" personally. (It was half a dozen sunflowers, with some nice purple statice mixed in for good measure. Mortified, I mumbled a "thanks" and hid them under the table.)

As women, we are either too visible, or made invisible. In meetings where my male partner Aner Ben-Ami and I are being pitched to, I'll often find that even if I ask a finance-related question, the entrepreneur or fund manager will in answering the question almost always make eye contact with him first, instead of with me. The instinct many people have to do this—finance-talk to the man, impact-talk to the woman—seems so automatic, ingrained, and subtle that it can go almost undetected. I'll note that this practice is common among both men and women—indeed, as women we are not immune to sexist practices either.

I've also learned that sexism and ageism have a unique kind of intersectionality. When I was the CEO of Toniic, and still in my mid-twenties, I was invited by a major bank to give a keynote presentation to their ultra-high-net-worth clientele at an exclusive resort in an even more exclusive ski town. I arrived to find ninety-eight men, one investor's wife, and me.

I learned that first evening to never again wear black to such an event. Two men came up to me to ask, "Excuse me ma'am, where's my table?" I'll confess, it took every ounce of my reserve not to say, "I'm your keynote—sit wherever the hell you want."

That particular night, I figured that behavior I'd first thought was sexist might simply be ageist—since in the investment world, ageism can apply to young people as much as it does to elders. Only two of the men attending were, like me, under forty, and the group seemed to ignore them, too. The three of us spent the whole evening together, perhaps in some unspoken solidarity. They turned out to be Biz Stone, cofounder of Twitter, and Shawn Bercuson, cofounder of Groupon. Clearly, our judgments about "who matters" in a room can sometimes cause us to miss opportunities to connect with amazing leaders.

But over the years, as I started to grow a head of gray hair that helped people understand it wasn't exactly my first day on the job, I realized that what I had often interpreted as ageism indeed really was sexism. I had a sad moment at one impact investment conference where I was sitting with five elder women and shared this observation, who confirmed that this had been their experience, too. I was shaken for weeks, saddened to think I couldn't "age out" of the sexism I was experiencing.

I know firsthand how frustrating—and alienating—being a woman in the industry can be, and I know how urgent it is that we as impact investors be more sensitive to issues of race and gender. I would argue that the long-term success of our industry depends on it. Indeed, not doing so is a huge business risk for a sector with a lot at stake in trying to prove that it can make acceptable returns. Not only do we risk simply reinforcing structures of injustice; we risk becoming irrelevant in a world where women and people of color are the majority.

If conventional wisdom is that investors work best analyzing areas they know, and the majority of people (and consumers) on the planet are women and people of color, we are likely to fail if we don't have teams that reflect that reality and broaden our personal exposure. For many years, working in mostly-white venues, I made an explicit point to get to know the people of color in the room. This was a very selfish move on my part: I knew these people had often worked twice as hard to be there, so they likely knew something I didn't—and also likely had access to networks and experiences very different from mine that I could learn from.

Sometimes, seeking out deeper connections in this way with people who do not look like me has felt uncomfortable. It's always difficult to meet new people, and it's even more difficult at events where people tend to self-segregate. And I certainly don't want to essentialize—to assume that a person can or should ever speak for a particular group. Everyone is an individual carrying multiple identities and influenced by many cultures and experiences. But I will say that many of my closest friends and successful investees are people I met when I got over the fear of my awkwardness and reached beyond my comfort zone. I am not telling my white readers to barge into the conversations of others; rather, perhaps begin by becoming more conscious of who you naturally gravitate toward in a room—who you see as "important," and why.

Over time, participating in all-white or male-dominated spaces may start to feel downright uncomfortable as well. As it becomes more and more clear that a major part of the population is missing from our conversations, how can we trust that our conclusions are good for the world?

Even corporate America is waking up to the fact that diverse teams and communities, whether based on race, gender, or other factors, simply create stronger businesses. Large corporations are now investing significant resources into diversity training and expanding their recruitment programs, among other activities intended to help build a more diverse workforce. This trend has made hiring even more challenging for white-led impact investment institutions, which now have to compete with the salary scales and resources corporations can provide, even if we do have the competitive advantage of providing a meaningful career that is increasingly attractive to millennials. If we don't catch up, we are in danger of falling behind as an industry. And, ideally, beyond merely diversifying established institutions, we can actively support, and invest in, new institutions being led by women and people of color.

This means that we need to be exceptionally conscious of what is sometimes referred to as "indirect discrimination"—policies that seem race and gender neutral that actually work in a discriminatory fashion. For instance, many investment firms have a policy of not supporting first-time funds, or ensuring that fund managers have a certain number of years of experience under their belts or have raised a certain amount of capital to be worthy of investment consideration. Given the fact that, as noted in the table, 98 percent of senior venture capitalists are white or Asian, and 92 percent are men, such rules actually do a *fantastic* job of excluding funds led by women or black or Latinx founders. As investors, rather than creating blanket exclusions, we need to be more creative and thoughtful in our underwriting—or we may very well miss out on opportunities to support exceptional emerging talent.[8]

7. Social Entrepreneurs Are Taught to Be Celebrity Business Leaders, Not Servant Leaders

People who want to become social entrepreneurs often go to an "incubator" or "accelerator" program for guidance and support, an experience that might last from a few weeks to six months; or perhaps they take a social enterprise course as part of their MBA curriculum. Regardless of the overall format, these programs typically include a week of instruction on how to manage cash flow, a week on marketing, and so on. But these same programs typically provide no training at all in community organizing and engagement. This process produces social entrepreneurs who can run great businesses, but who, like the aid workers before them, lack the cultural competency and exposure to really build supportive communities that can drive transformative change. Additionally, these programs need to explore methodologies that will respect and uphold effective community leadership models already in place, rather than asking communities that are more accustomed to these collective structures to simply adopt Western business models.

Case in point: I remember once meeting with an entrepreneur at an elite business school who had invented a fascinating technology to generate electricity in rural areas, and was receiving ample support from his university to promote his efforts. I asked him about the user testing he had done so far. He said that during his spring break, he had driven down to Mexico with his girlfriend to do some field-testing in between their sight-seeing. I cringed as I asked my next question, but something in his manner made it clear I should ask: "Do you speak Spanish?"

"Well, no . . . but I watched them use the product."

Beyond a qualitative study of smiles, it was hard to imagine how much useful data was going to emerge through this sort of "field-testing." This entrepreneur, like so many others, had focused on building a solution before having any contact with everyday people to see what problems, if any, they might want solved by outsiders.

Although his technology may very well make money, an enterprise that lacks a deep connection with the community it purports to serve has no way to evaluate whether it is actually successful as a *social* enterprise. This leads to far too many individuals who want to be social entrepreneurs going out in search of a problem that fits the solution they already have in mind, rather than truly learning what's needed and then responding accordingly.

"Market-based solutions" are said to have a distinct advantage in terms of impact assessment over giveaways, because the fact that poor people are willing to buy the product is the ultimate test of its usefulness. However, going back to concern number three, about taking "easy wins" through incremental progress, all this can really prove is that what is being offered is slightly better than the terrible, exploitative alternative that has been offered in the past. Or perhaps it is a transformational intervention, but the market itself is not enough to tell you that. An entrepreneur who is an island, selling his technology to people with whom he or she interacts only as consumers, is limiting his or her potential for transformative activity.

Instead of being servant leaders and building community, entrepreneurs are too often implicitly expected to model the cult of personality in order to succeed and attract capital: to be at the center, the one person with the idea that will change the world, who hustles and sacrifices to get it done; who, if he or she is lucky, will not only get a filmed TED Talk but perhaps a spot on the *Today Show*. Many entrepreneurs aren't natural attention seekers and don't like having to play this particular role on the public stage, but doing so is often considered essential to leading a successful enterprise.

The social entrepreneur does have a crucial role to play, and there's nothing wrong with leveraging a dynamic personality to attract attention to a cause. But an entrepreneur can often do more by leading from behind than by carrying the torch him or herself, and ideally, this style of leadership would be better appreciated by the investment community.

It became apparent to me that the investment community was failing to recognize the value of this kind of servant leadership when I started applying for social enterprise fellowships back in 2011. One organization with a particularly prestigious, six-figure fellowship had a list of prequalifying questions on its online submission form—the type where if you don't check yes you are not allowed to proceed. One such question was, "Are you, or you and your co-founder, the sole originators of this idea and enterprise?" At the time I was part of an organization with five cofounders—but I had no choice but to check yes in order to fill out the full application.

When I was asked later in the process to give our founding story, I answered the question by saying, "We are a community of five cofounders, thirty founding members, and countless advisors. Anyone who tries to start an organization completely alone is an idiot, and you should not invest in them." We made it to the next round.

In social justice organizations, having distributed leadership is often viewed as essential—not only from the perspective of democratic decision-making and rebalancing of historical inequities, but also to ensure better decisions and long-term continuity, period. In social enterprise, too much emphasis is placed on the infallible entrepreneur who wants to do nothing else with his or her life and will do anything to make it happen. And yet, most social investments are expected to last for seven years or more—an unfathomable amount of time for the average twenty-five-year-old entrepreneur. If the business rests solely on the entrepreneur's shoulders, without the support of others who are equally invested in its success, it is likely to have trouble meeting the inevitable challenges that will appear down the road. Whether or not you care about social business per se, going solo is simply a major business risk.

One of my friends and longtime mentors is Billy Parish, founder of the Energy Action Coalition, a nonprofit student network, and Mosaic, a solar company. Billy understood these concepts intrinsically and hence is a fantastic serial entrepreneur. He was nominated as "activist of the year" by *Vogue* magazine in 2009, and *Vogue* was planning to feature an article about him and nine others who had earned this honor. Each was to have a smiling headshot and bio published in the print magazine, which is distributed to more than 1 million people monthly.

But Energy Action was a *coalition*, and Billy insisted to *Vogue* that all forty of its leaders at the time be allowed to pose with him for the picture. *Vogue* ultimately agreed, and the final spread showed nine full-sized, polished individuals . . . and one group of forty. Billy prioritized collective responsibility and acknowledgment over his own ego, and that's how he built an organization that has stood the test of time. His latest startup, Mosaic, recently raised a $220 million private equity round, and it is thriving under his servant-leadership style.

8. Social Education Is Not Being Taken as Seriously as Financial Education

The industry treats social knowledge as extracurricular—something "nice to have" that can be learned and assessed intuitively, rather than a "must have" that requires ongoing education and effort.

If someone wants to become an investor with access to significant resources, there is a relatively clear pathway for how to do so: get a degree in economics or math or statistics or business from a well-regarded college or university. Do two years in consulting or at an investment bank before going back for an MBA at another well-regarded institution. Intern for a private equity firm or investment bank, then start working as an investment manager. If you wake up one day deciding, "I'd like to do well by doing good," the impact investment field is available to you as a lateral shift, either within an impact-oriented fund or by moving into the impact unit of your particular institution (for instance, the social finance department of J. P. Morgan, Cambridge Associates, or Deutsche Bank, to name a few). In this typical scenario, it takes at least six years of financial training to feel qualified as an investor, and that is entirely appropriate: investing is tough and high-stakes work.

What is the equivalent of social training appropriate to becoming an impact investor? Is social change not equally tough and high-stakes?

I would ask any investor aspiring to move into the impact field to think deeply about what kind of social training and ongoing education you'll need to be effective in your role, even if your institution never explicitly requires it. What would be the social education equivalent of the six-year program you'd undertake for a typical investment job? Who will you turn to for current information? How can you build that network just as you would for any other subject area or investment focus? The answers are far from clear, but rather than putting the burden on each individual investor to figure it out, the industry needs to decide that impact education is a priority and build the necessary systems and structures. It's an issue that requires collective thinking and action.

It's also worth noting that we will *never* be experts on someone else's lived experiences. Getting a two-year master's degree in social change may make you more aware, but it still doesn't qualify you to make decisions on behalf of others. That is why we have to build structures to be in relationship with global communities, not just add a "social" course to MBA programs. How do we establish accountability structures as an industry so we can make sure that what we think of as impact is actually providing what people need and want?

Despite devoting their lives and talents to trying to deploy resources responsibly around the globe, philanthropists and aid workers have in many cases failed to identify and scale effective interventions. The grassroots activists and social movements really have us beat from this perspective—their main assets being knowledge, lived experience, and strength in numbers, not dollars. As investors we should be so lucky to learn from them.

Learning about social change is not as simple as it seems. It's a constantly evolving subject that changes as quickly as anything else in the world.

For example, I generally consider myself to be fairly up-to-date on the LGBTQ rights movement. I was part of the Gay Straight Alliance (GSA, a national movement) in high school, and afterward remained as reasonably well-informed and well-educated as any Bay Area progressive, wrestling with my own identity, following the news and trying to be a supportive friend to people around me.

My best friend from middle school came out as transgender just after high school, and my father used to ask me very politely about how my "transsexual" friend was doing. With a daughter's usual impatience, I would roll my eyes and say, "Dad! Don't say transsexual. That's insulting. The preferred term is transgendered."*

I was sharing this anecdote with Rashad Robinson, a friend of mine who is the executive director of Color Of Change, an online advocacy organization concerned with strengthening the black political voice, with over 600,000 members. I told him the story mostly to illustrate the point that well-meaning people may not always have the right language to be effective allies, even if their hearts are absolutely in the right place. My father didn't have the terminology right, but his care for my childhood friend was sincere. We can only find that sincerity is in fact there if we don't completely write people off at their first word-choice slip.

---

*Currently, "transgender" is more commonly used than "transgendered," which can be considered an insult because it implies that something externally happened to the person rather than the idea that the person is asserting an identity. I use "transgendered" in this anecdote because at the time it was Lucian's preferred term. (And yes—that's Lucian Kahn, future frontman of the Jewish comedy band Schmekel.) I checked in with Lucian in the process of writing, who noted, "In 2000–2001, the community of people I knew were using 'transgender' and 'transgendered' interchangeably, and also used 'tranny' as an in-group term of endearment, like a reclaimed slur similar to the current use of 'queer.' When I came out the second time in 2010, the community of people I knew were mostly using 'trans.' Sometimes they used 'transgender' in formal contexts. Use of the word 'transgendered' was now regarded as ignorant. By 2013, almost everyone I knew considered 'tranny' a seriously offensive slur." Which goes back to the point of this anecdote . . . it takes real paying attention as the world evolves!

He laughed and said, "You're right. . . . By the way, did you know more recently 'transsexual' has made a comeback? Because sex is the biological term, whereas gender is a socially constructed concept." He had worked at a prominent LGBTQ rights organization before joining Color Of Change, and as a gay man he was far more attuned to the world's shifts in terminology than I was. Apparently my retro-dad was now right, and I was the one who needed a linguistic adjustment.

I'm not sure what term my childhood friend currently prefers, but let's say I could easily have offended him by using the wrong one. In the same way, some well-meaning activists offended others by saying All Lives Matter, as they failed to consider that Black Lives Matter has a completely different meaning, because the idea that white lives matter was never in question. No one worries that people saying "Save the Rainforest" don't care about other forests. One has to pay a great deal of attention to really take direction from affected communities. It takes deep relationships and trust to talk about some very painful and vulnerable subjects. And while some people may point to sensitivity around linguistic precision as evidence of the repressive force of "political correctness," it's hard to imagine that we can effectively build bridges if we don't pay attention to using language that feels accurate and safe to the people with whom we want to connect. Language is just the start—then the actual conversation begins.

Ask fund managers how they get their social education alongside their investment education, and you'd be amazed how many are rattled and surprised by the question. Typically, they simply haven't thought about it, and have to take a moment away from their usual pitch script to come up with an answer. So far I have had two investment managers say they read the *New York Times*. Others have said they rely on other team members. Then there's the most common response: "Impact: you just know it when you see it."

This line is a fantastic way to evade responsibility for being as disciplined about one's ongoing social education as about one's financial education. How can you *possibly* know it, when you don't even actually see it? Impact investors based in the Global North often have limited opportunities to spend time in developing countries, and certainly not to live among the poor, but, at best, merely go to visit them for a few hours before returning to the offices of investees. Or perhaps they do invest within their own country, but with limited connections to the social groups they intend to serve. It's not because these people don't care—they do, deeply. It's because, as they go about doing their jobs as financial managers, they often lack the time or the freedom to be on the ground more often. Their jobs are structurally focused on the investor *client* more than on the beneficiary.

I also sometimes feel that the surprise I encounter in response to this question is a reflection of how gender roles are often still divided within the impact investment industry. All things social are considered to be "soft skill" related, a euphemism for "women's work," whereas the men handle the quantitative, "hard skill" investment activity. In a very unscientific review, I've seen that when a fund hires an impact manager, that manager is almost inevitably a woman. This means that impact management is outsourced to one person rather than being considered integral to the investment operations of the entire team; it is thought to be more art than science, and like all arts, is considered feminine, and thus implicitly devalued. Especially in the context of a historically male-dominated field, we cannot waste time and energy writing off impact as "women's work."

At the end of the day, yes, the activists should go get their MBAs if they want to be investors and entrepreneurs, but the investors, in turn, should be taking their two years out in the field, and maintaining consistent relationships with social movements. This type of training and experience is necessary if they want to be truly effective and earn their title as impact investors. If we cannot construct an industry where time in country and in community is feasible for investors, then perhaps we should focus more on impact investing in the Global North, developing strong relationships at home, and supporting the development of local teams in the Global South.

THE WAY FORWARD

With this laundry list of challenges in hand, where do we go from here? If we don't have all the right answers, can we at least make sure to ask the right questions?

This is a critical point, and it's why this book is not a finger-pointing diatribe. Because the problem isn't that we have bad actors doing evil things to the poor and the planet: it's that we have a field composed of tremendously dedicated, well-meaning people, who are very committed to social change, but who are often focusing on the wrong questions. If we can shift the industry to focus on a better set of questions, my hope is that we will achieve better long-term outcomes that we all can be proud of. Knowing that perfection is unattainable, what structures will enable us to be flexible over time in a way that is accountable to affected communities? The next chapters show what these processes can look like, and how they can ultimately lead us toward greater transformative change.

four

SCALING SMART

AROUND THE SAME TIME THAT I STARTED TO DEVELOP misgivings about impact investment, the world started to catch on to its incredible potential. All the buzz in the industry was about finally "mainstreaming." In 2010 J. P Morgan issued the influential report *Impact Investments: An Emerging Asset Class*, projecting that the impact investment industry was primed to produce up to $667 billion in profits over the next decade.[1] That amount of investment would constitute ten times as much as official development aid globally if the pace of aid remained steady—although, with "market-based solutions" to ending poverty increasingly in vogue, the future of traditional aid itself was becoming shaky.

The J. P. Morgan report was tremendously exciting to those of us who had dedicated our careers to the promise of impact investment, not only because of the huge numbers it projected, but because it signified that major financial institutions were finally taking note and preparing to become leaders in the field. It was also, of course, *terrifying*.

We were going to rapidly scale an industry that was riddled with flaws, and we were going to supplant an aid industry that had suffered from very similar logistical and ethical challenges. The seductiveness of the idea that there is a magic-bullet solution to poverty that we can latch on to and scale can make antipoverty approaches as trendy as sneakers. Billions of dollars get deployed for so-called solutions that eventually get abandoned when they are later deemed ineffective—either because the solution never really worked in the first place, or because it got perverted as it scaled. Is this the inevitable path of impact investment? What do we need to get right from the start, to make sure we scale the right thing?

Almost everything published about impact investment to that point, particularly by practitioners, was overwhelmingly positive. Practitioners and their admirers wanted to show off the incredible financial returns as well as the social impact such investments were achieving in order to establish legitimacy, and define an industry that was still getting on its feet. I knew this was essential work, and I was excited myself to see all the case studies—coming from investors as diverse as pension funds and foundations—proving that investors didn't need to sacrifice their values in order to have positive financial outcomes. I wanted new entrants, and more money, to come into the field and, as much as anyone, I wanted society to move away from fossil fuels, private prisons, and sweatshops, and do so as quickly as possible.

Still, my questions about the industry nagged at me. I was concerned that very few people seemed to be having meaningful conversations about our industry's challenges, and were instead focusing simply on acceptance and scale. I felt like a naysayer, even though all I was saying was, "Hey, as we scale the industry, let's make sure we get it right!" The classic response was, essentially, some version of, "This industry just got started. Shhhh—don't criticize it or we won't get to scale!"

This reluctance to acknowledge the "naysayers" within the field made it difficult for us to hold critical, meaningful conversations, and I began to feel increasingly alone as I tried to explore questions about how to enhance impact investment's real impact potential. I was afraid I'd wake up in twenty years and find out that our field had made people worse off.

I know that, as an investor, talking about fairness can sometimes make me seem like a real Pollyanna—a vestige of my five-year-old self screaming "*It's not fair!*" in the face of an economy that was never designed to be fair. If we can make a million people better off, isn't that good and important? Yes. But wouldn't it be better if we structurally ensured that all people in the transaction gained what they deserved, not just what was better than what they had before? Also yes.

I worry that in the quest for scale, it's all too easy to let the impact be good . . . but not good *enough* to avoid replicating cycles of extraction from communities. To me, that means accepting a level of modest change when what the world needs is immediate action and fundamental structural change. While we should celebrate the progress achieved through incremental change, it is intellectually lazy to be content with anything less than fundamental change, and reflects a lack of accountability to the people we claim to be serving in our work.

I believe we can successfully scale impact investment such that it reflects principles of fairness and accountability. But it's going to require a broader shift in consciousness.

The debate about how best to conduct and scale impact investment is a legitimate one. There are many investors who in their desire for speed and breadth of impact take an approach that's different from mine, and I still respect them deeply for their commitment to social change. I was on a hike at a Toniic gathering with one such investor, Mark Straub, who leads Khosla Impact. Khosla's focus is investing in businesses that have the power to impact at least a million people.[2] Instead of following a strict, limiting definition for impact, it has a general focus on businesses that improve standards of living in emerging markets. Mark challenged me for making it my priority to figure out a model for intervention that was exactly right and perfectly fair, asking whether I shouldn't just focus on helping more people. He's my favorite type of thinker—one who makes you feel you need a notebook and a nap after a conversation.

At one point Mark shared the old adage, "Don't let the perfect be the enemy of the good." I stopped on the trail to think for a moment, and then shouted, with only a tinge of irony, "Mark, I *am* the enemy of the good!"

Being the enemy of the good—meaning, in this case, an advocate for something better and more transformative—is a tough role to play in an industry where everyone truly is motivated by the idea of doing good. My hope is that by innovating new models *that also can scale*, we can truly maximize our potential and our sense of possibility for the field. We shouldn't let the best be the enemy of the good—but at the same time, we shouldn't let the good be the enemy of the best, either.

I believe that activists and advocates of impact investment will choose systemic change over palliative change if they are given a proven, practical option. In our work, we often support opportunities that are scaling well in sectors we care about, then also support more community-oriented, sometimes smaller-scale, and typically earlier-stage solutions that can help to shift what that sector actually does in the long run. So it's not completely fair to say I'm the enemy of the good—I just want the good to be challenged by the best!

A commitment to fairness need not be mistaken for something radical and impossibly idealistic. For further confirmation that fairness is a viable objective, take a look at an organization that takes an approach far more conservative than mine—the Rotary Club. Since 1933, the Rotary Club has asked its 1.2 million members globally to take this "Four-Way Test" before executing any action:

1. Is it the truth?
2. Is it fair to all concerned?
3. Will it build goodwill and better friendships?
4. Will it be beneficial to all concerned?

In the next chapter I will introduce the Transform Finance principles, my best attempt to similarly articulate a set of guiding ideas to help us scale impact investment with a clear commitment to transformative change and the pursuit of fairness. Whether these are the right ones, or if others should replace them, is a subject I hope practitioners, activists, and anyone interested in a better world will debate in the coming years.

What I am sure of is that the pursuit of scale should be accompanied by a litmus test to make sure we are continuing on the right path.

LESSONS FROM MICROFINANCE

For a vivid, cautionary tale about what can happen when financial scale is pursued without an equally strong commitment to a set of social principles, we have only to review the history of microfinance. The impact investment field has tried to disassociate itself from the increasingly bad rep of the microfinance world over the past few years, but, as they say of Cuba and Puerto Rico, despite their differences on the surface we cannot fail to acknowledge they are "two wings of the same bird." Most accounting of impact investment's size as a field still includes microfinance, and microfinance is likely to be a dominant piece of the industry for some time, given its well-developed commercial infrastructure.

Since microfinance is perhaps the closest corollary to impact investment that we have in terms of its original intentions, it's worth considering the history of the field in depth to see what lessons we can learn from its trajectory. I don't want to dwell too long on the now decades-old debate over whether microfinance works as an antipoverty intervention—what's more important in shaping impact investment's future is to examine closely *how it scaled*, what choices were made along the way, and how those choices affected the industry's potential for lasting positive social and economic impact.

Microfinance follows the basic principle that "it takes money to make money." In many small business contexts, particularly those led by women, a lack of capital leads to economically inefficient choices—for instance, a woman might have to buy ten-packs of toilet paper to then sell them as individual rolls in her village, because she cannot afford to buy the much cheaper (by unit) pack of one hundred, which would have enabled her to have a higher profit margin, and perhaps move from earning $2 a day to $5, just scraping over the poverty line. Or maybe she sells eggs, and a second chicken could double her income—and yet it's always hard to save up enough to purchase that other chicken. Providing small amounts of capital to either current or aspiring entrepreneurs whose businesses were too small or who lived too remotely to be reached by banks was a very effective intervention, particularly when loans were provided for productive purposes.

So it sounds good in principle—and it is good! Microfinance, like agriculture, health, education, or any number of sectors, is not inherently good or bad. It's execution that matters, and it's a combination of structure and execution that will determine just how much impact a particular intervention is destined to have. No one solution will be a panacea, either. In the best cases, microfinance can be a critical element of income development and an engine of innovation for emerging economies. By diversifying from just credit to include savings and insurance, and ensuring responsible uses of credit for both enterprises and individual consumers, financial services can help address the "poverty penalty" paid in overpriced goods, limited ability to take on risk (and opportunity), and overpriced capital in times of emergency.

Microfinance is one element in a suite of efforts that must be made to support the livelihoods of the global poor, alongside government policy and quality job creation. It must be acknowledged as a "micro" solution to what is generally a "macro" structural problem: the lack of opportunity in emerging markets. However, a "pulling yourself up by the bootstraps" narrative, with microfinance as the solution, ignores the structural deficiencies that often keep people poor despite their best individual efforts, and from that perspective microfinance can reinforce a very dangerous narrative that the West has used to blame the victim—not only internationally, but at home as well—when entrepreneurial efforts fail.

It's hard to imagine macroeconomic development happening in a country without a financial system that works for all of its citizens. And that's part of why, ideally, microfinance is indeed micro*finance*—involving not just microloans or credit, but a whole suite of financial services that, like the invention of paper money, make the process of using resources to build more resources a little more efficient. Communities have practiced some form of microfinance—from savings circles to farmers co-ops—essentially since humans first settled into communities and began to grow their own food, and many grassroots groups still advocate for fair access to affordable credit as a major objective.

There are two major debates in particular about microfinance that can help us think about similar questions getting raised about impact investment.

First, does microfinance help people, and if so, how much? Depending on who you talk to about microfinance, it is either the solution to global poverty and deserves to be included in the basic list of human rights, or it's a complete rip-off of the global poor that only serves to concentrate more resources in the hands of the wealthy. A long line of studies have been unable to prove the point for either side, but the question is useful nonetheless in determining how much time and effort to invest in this intervention versus others.

Second, should microfinance make money, and if so, how much? One school of thought held that, for microfinance to scale and attract and maintain commercial capital, it needed to show that it could achieve market rates of return. Others believed that, if it was truly a social intervention, perhaps it shouldn't make money beyond enabling institutions to sustain themselves—especially if the ownership of those institutions was concentrated among outside, historically wealthy parties.

There is a clear and often underacknowledged interaction between the elements addressed by these two debates. If our starting place in defining successful scale-up is the achievement of a certain expected return for the investor, then the tail is likely to wag the dog in terms of the types of financial services provided to communities under the banner of microfinance. It's no accident, for example, that many microfinance institutions have promoted loans far more than they have promoted savings, as the margins are much better on loans—and in the case of some less scrupulous institutions, people have been flat-out prohibited from opening savings accounts if they are not taking out a loan as well. The assumption became, "Microfinance works, so let's scale it"—without acknowledging how scaling could actually change the nature of microfinance.

Ultimately, scaling up became the predominant preoccupation and ambition for the industry before the questions of "Does it actually work, and under what circumstances does it work best?" were fully answered. Where microfinance went wrong was not just in prioritizing scale over impact, but in relying on the financial markets in their current format to achieve that scale.

Our current financial system is really fantastic and efficient at scaling things that are exceptionally profitable, at least in the context of a very short-term view of profitability. But managing institutions toward profitability above and beyond everything else has consequences for everyday people.

Early adopters of microfinance wanted to prove that it was a commercially viable product, and that it deserved space in your portfolio alongside real estate and the stock market. By

2010, they had succeeded. Compartamos Banco, a Mexican
bank largely owned by Accion International, had been able
to undertake an initial public offering (IPO) in 2007 with a
valuation ultimately reaching $1.5 billion, implying a 250x
return on the initial $6 million put in by founding share-
holders, a roughly 100 percent annual return compounded
over eight years.[3] It was one of the world's highest-grossing
IPOs in a year when the market was otherwise in havoc due
to the machinations of yet another financial innovation gone
rogue—mortgages. In 2010, in India, the microfinance institution SKS also went through an IPO that generated millions
in profits—-along with an impressive amount of scandal and
intrigue. In both cases, a large number of shares (and in the
case of Compartamos, the majority of shares) were owned by
nonprofit institutions, which presumably plowed this profit
back into more development work.

Globally, some $38 billion in investments and 624 million
"beneficiaries" later, microfinance had indeed grown up as an
industry.[4] But while the industry was scaling so effectively, it
had a rougher time justifying its popularity based on the idea
that it was actually helping poor people. A 1998 study by Mark
M. Pitt and Shahidur R. Khandker that inspired elation about
microfinance's impact on poverty was later discredited by David Roodman, a well-known research scientist in the field,
as having been based on faulty methodology.[5] Additionally,
Grameen, the bank founded by Muhammad Yunus that had
pioneered microfinance, issued a literature review in 2010 of
the most thoroughly conducted randomized controlled trials
at the time. The report concluded that "collectively, these three
studies suggest that microfinance had impacts on business investment and outcomes, *but did not have impacts (positive or*

negative) on broader measures of poverty and social well-being"
(my emphasis). The only positive impact, according to the
study, was that people who already had higher incomes and
established businesses were able to benefit from access to financial services.[6] When I did my own review of the literature
and spent a month interviewing microfinance experts, essentially trying my hardest to build an argument for microfinance
and fill up a PowerPoint slide with success stories, I had to
stop at three bullet points—the data simply wasn't there.

So where did the impact go? When you prioritize profitability over impact, whether in microfinance or otherwise, in the
worst cases it can leave already poor people heavily indebted
and enhance the poverty penalty of their economic activities.
It can also lead to heavily extractive institutions providing
only marginal levels of benefit, as they will choose to provide
activities and services according to which ones are most profitable, rather than which best support poor people. If they
limit their activities to microloans and microcredit, focusing
on the deployment of debt rather than debt as just one potential tool for asset-building, then it's tough to imagine poor
people being able to get ahead. And if the ownership structure
of microfinance institutions is not addressed alongside profitability, then the institutions become by nature extractive, removing money in the form of payments from one historically
under-resourced community and providing it to another to
continue the process of capital accumulation for themselves.

Note that the most salient issue here is not interest rates.
Most critics of microfinance focus on the fact that institutions
charge poor borrowers interest rates upward of 60 percent,
or even 200 percent in the most extreme cases. But in some
regions of the world, high rates may be quite appropriate to

match what it takes to even reach a client, as the organization simply needs to hire a more extensive team or take on more risk. The more important metric to track is profitability to outside stakeholders—the quantity of excess resources that are created that are not then deployed to further support the client community—and whether this number is reasonable compared to the value created for clients.

Many advocates of microfinance will say that the fact that poor people voluntarily choose to take a high-interest loan proves that it's useful to them, and that one must trust that the poor are rational actors who know their best interests more than anyone else. I agree, and indeed, poor people may still choose to take a deal that is fundamentally extractive—because their next best alternative is so incredibly awful, not because what is being offered otherwise is particularly desirable or fair. But if a financial institution doesn't add more value than it extracts, then by nature it cannot systemically change outcomes for the poor or successfully challenge inequality on a societal level.

Yunus himself eventually published an editorial in the *New York Times* asserting that his intention had been for microfinance to reach sustainability and grow accordingly, not for it to become wildly profitable, and that he was disappointed with the path the industry had taken, a move showing exceptional humility and leadership on his part.[7] He thought microfinance institutions should not need to maintain more than 10 to 15 percent profitability to run their operations and reward investors. Similarly, and perhaps more conservatively, Damian von Stauffenberg, founder of MicroRate, the first ratings agency devoted to evaluating performance and risk in microfinance institutions, went on record saying that microfinance loan pricing should not be 20 to 30 percent more expensive than prevailing rates, and that profitability should be limited to 30 percent.[8]

The microfinance industry, recognizing that it was facing some serious threats to its reputation, implemented several regulation programs, such as the Smart Campaign, which aimed to ensure transparency in interest rates, enforce scrupulous collection standards, and otherwise protect clients from unsavory practices. Given the lack of independence these programs have from the industry they supposedly regulate, however, many thoughtful impact investors fear accidentally investing in products that are actually harming people even when they claim or aspire to follow the stated principles (a practice sometimes referred to as "impact-washing"). This is generally not due to any maliciousness, but simply the challenge of managing large portfolios across multiple countries without sufficient presence on the ground. Although the industry is still strongly capitalized by financial markets, this risk has rendered it less attractive to impact investors. Ironically, impact investors sometimes confess that they keep microfinance products in their portfolios for the profile of investment return they can generate, rather than for the love of the impact they promise.

The existence of these regulatory programs makes microfinance banks resemble any bank in a screened impact portfolio: presume the bank is largely good when it conducts business as usual, then regulate it to ensure it doesn't do anything too terrible. Note that this kind of "let the market do its thing, then regulate it" philosophy reflects *exactly* the kind of thinking impact investment is supposed to rectify. Simply putting regulatory fences around "old economy" practices, and expanding their reach to new audiences, is not the same thing as creating new ways of doing business and building a more equitable economy.

Yunus's response to profiteering in the microlending industry has been to promote the concept of "social business," by which he means businesses formed expressly for social purposes that do not take profits out of communities, which is quite different from the way other actors globally tend to define a social business (as just any business that makes profit and helps people along the way).[9] The term sheet for the Grameen Crédit Agricole Fund, for instance, actually states that investors are expected to use all the profits they make from their investment in the fund for future social purposes. It's a tough term to enforce, but an interesting one to think about.[10]

Unlike his work in microfinance, which spread like wildfire, Yunus's social business concept has not achieved the same level of recognition. People perceive it as promoting impact investment without profitability: a nonstarter for most people. I view this interpretation as a fundamental misreading of Yunus's concept. The point isn't to take profitability out of social business; it's to be very careful and thoughtful about the distribution and use of profits among the different players in the system.

Some important actors in the microfinance field, such as the GAWA Microfinance Fund, Global Partnerships, and MicroCredit Enterprises, have taken real steps to put impact first in their practices and in the choices they make about which institutions they support, and their efforts should be applauded and supported. Microfinance is still an important tool for development. Rather than just throwing it out of the portfolio, impact investors should support the institutions that are getting it back on track.

And as we continue to scale the impact investment field as a whole, we should make sure to absorb the lessons of the failures of microfinance rather than trying to disassociate from them. Indeed, there are lessons from microfinance we can take to heart. The scaling pathway of microfinance looked roughly like this:

1. Identify a good idea that seems to work in helping poor people get to a better standard of living.
2. Figure out which elements make it profitable.
3. Scale those first and foremost.
4. Try to regulate those elements after the new industry experiences backlash.
5. Lose the interest of the impact investment community as its members lose faith in the ability to actually help poor people, but continue scaling using largely commercial capital.

Now just imagine, for a moment, what might happen if we did things differently:

1. Identify a good idea that has a mix of qualitative and quantitative, micro and macro approaches to addressing poverty and structural inequality.
2. Design a system to hold that idea accountable to the people it intends to serve, and that allows it to be flexible and adaptive in response to lessons learned on the ground.
3. Define an appropriate level of profitability, and pay attention to the proportion of profits reinvested in

the communities that created those profits, relative to those taken out of those communities.

4. Scale appropriately.

Making something wildly profitable will of course attract the attention of financial markets, and thus wild profitability becomes a very efficient way to scale a financial instrument. Sometimes, however, the elements that make something profitable might not be the elements that are most essential to having a positive social impact. So it's important to recognize that if we expect to expand impact investment based primarily on its profitability, we should expect to get just what we set out to create: a tool that has maximized the axis of profit, but with a lagging axis of impact.

The question then becomes, How else do we scale? What is the most efficient nexus point of profitability and impact? I believe we can organize the industry around a new set of questions so that we can figure this out together.

So rather than asking, "How do we scale fastest?"—the answer being, "Rely on conventional financial markets, even if that perverts our original purpose"—what if we ask a slightly different question: "What is an appropriate model for scaling an industry, a model that will actually make the world a more equitable and sustainable place?"

Will developing this model, whatever it is, mean sacrificing some scale in the short term? Probably, yes. Is that a worthwhile tradeoff, if it means that economic systems actually shift for the long term? These are the questions that I hope we can keep debating as we take advantage of our current opportunity to do better in scaling impact investment.

five

HOW TO GET IT RIGHT

A S I GAINED MORE EXPERIENCE IN IMPACT INVESTING, and more exposure to the challenges and questions facing the field, I found myself in a major quandary. Would impact investment just replicate the errors of charity and build a top-down industry that solved problems for investors rather than for communities? Or could these issues be addressed, such that impact investment could fulfill a vision of community autonomy? Was there space to make social justice considerations truly an integral part of how the field developed? Or did I need to find a new instrument for change?

At this point, I had more than a decade of experience in the impact investment industry. I still believed deeply in its potential; I had the contacts to navigate it effectively; and I didn't want to give up. So rather than abandoning impact investment, I spent the next few years working to discover new approaches to make it realize its potential—and finding ways to scale smart.

A NEW VISION FOR IMPACT

If I wanted to figure out what to scale, I needed to first take some of my own medicine, and make sure to have frontline communities in the global fight for their livelihoods and the natural environment at the table to inform my strategy and terms of engagement.

In 2011 I attended the World Social Forum in Dakar, a gathering of over 75,000 social activists from around the globe that happens every two years and that is about as grassroots as one can get while still having a foot in the nonprofit world.

Women's groups one hundred members strong had bused in from Mali and the Gambia; farmers from Mexico and Brazil came; there were people from just about every possible social stratum. A donors contingent organized by the EDGE Funders Alliance Network, a progressive community of more than 150 foundations and individuals devoted to effective philanthropy, also attended, but as far as I could tell, there was no one there from the impact investment community at all beyond my lone delegation of one.

I spent much of my time hanging out at the tent of La Via Campesina, a global peasants movement that had representatives attending from about fifteen countries across Asia, Latin America, and Africa. In a cacophony of languages (and through a lot of patient translation), we shared challenges, tactics, and some incredible stories over those five days.

These activists were incredibly sophisticated. They knew the ins and outs of every World Bank and UN deal. They had analyzed capital flows and contributed to the design of social and environmental policies for global institutions. They could explain the difference between sustainable agriculture, organic agriculture, and agroecology, and the business models and collaboration between government and farmers essential for each.

I asked them, "How is impact investing affecting your community?"

To my surprise, this global trend that was about to eclipse aid and redefine how the Global South received its funding—no one had even heard of it. They had no idea that "socially purposed" funds were behind some of the agricultural deals that were the source of land grabs, or were funding businesses that paid poverty wages. They were appalled at the wrong-headedness of these projects—but simultaneously intrigued. These funds, they recognized, could conceivably also be used to support their efforts for autonomy and development on their own terms.

While those of us in the Global North had been developing the practice of impact investment, activists in the Global South, who could have helped shape the field's future and improve its trajectory, had been largely missing from the conversation.

My philosophy as a white US activist has always been to spend as much time listening as possible, especially since I know that in some circles my presence alone can shift the dynamic of a conversation. So in spaces like the World Social Forum, I rarely presented unless asked; in general I barely spoke unless spoken to. But this was one of those moments when I realized I needed to step up and, by sharing what I knew about impact investment, help bring new voices into the fold.

After engaging in a number of one-on-one conversations to get a better sense of how the current state of impact investment applied to the struggles these leaders were facing, I invited some of the participants to meet in a loaned tent at 3:00 p.m. on the last day of the conference. I had no idea if people would show up—knowing that they had already gone through five days of exhausting conversation, I didn't expect much, especially at an event where literally dozens of activities were going on simultaneously.

Approximately twenty-five people showed up from four continents, enough that we had to go get some extra chairs from a neighboring tent. The participants represented constituencies ranging from a couple of hundred people (like the EDGE Funders) to a couple of million (like La Via Campesina). That felt like enough to me to talk about starting a movement.

I gave a basic overview of impact investment, where it was going, and the challenges I saw it facing. I then invited the circle to comment on how they had experienced these challenges in their local environment, and also to share their visions of how the impact investment world could best support the dreams of their constituents.

We stayed in that tent for three hours as the energy built and ideas kept flowing. At the end of it we formed a small working group to continue to drive the work forward, and then headed off to an inspiring speech by Evo Morales, the Bolivian president and closing presenter for the conference.

My memory of who exactly was at that first meeting and who exactly said what is vague. But I do remember the feeling I had, and that I believe we all shared, of an overwhelming conviction that impact investment could be a tremendous tool for community autonomy, and that if we were able to host a broader conversation about how it could grow, we could leave the era of aid dependency in the past and move on into a new global economy that works for everyday people. Not one that was perfect, of course—but one that would have much more broadly distributed leadership and access to resources.

Out of this meeting came a small, global group of activists, from Egypt, Mozambique, Mexico, India, and the United States, who volunteered to help me craft a vision for the organization that would eventually become Transform Finance. As a first step we needed to establish some clear principles that could effectively guide a movement and inspire aligned investors.

Our criteria for our guiding principles included the following:

» They had to be relatable at a heart-level, such that they would resonate internally to anyone reading them regardless of that reader's political perspective. A person's first response to reading our principles needed to be, "Yes, of course I want that. . . . Who wouldn't?"

» They had to be inherently actionable, and imply their own course of action. I have seen groups put forward guiding principles like, "Respect the dignity of all people"—indeed, a great goal, but one that few know how to implement consistently. This meant as well that they had to be measurable and verifiable; since, as they say in business, what gets measured, gets managed.

» They had to be applicable across sectors and geographies, so that there wouldn't be an easy excuse to "opt out." (Although at the end of the day nothing can be 100 percent universally applicable, we did our best.)

» We capped the number of principles at three—enough to have some real meaning, but not so many that a listener would tune out before you could finish your elevator pitch.

Taking these instructions to heart, I landed on the following three principles:

1. *Engage communities in design, governance, and ownership.* This principle was a response to seeing communities being treated only as inputs—that is, labor—or as consumers, rather than being given an opportunity to participate in all stages of enterprise development and management as well as in long-term value creation through ownership.

2. *Add more value than you extract.* This principle is perhaps my favorite, because it's the most heart-intuitive—Who really wants to extract value from the poor? It was inspired by Brendan Martin, who had pioneered the concept of nonextractive finance over the previous decade.

3. *Fairly balance risk and return between investors, entrepreneurs, and communities.* Once again, I expected that people would respond on an emotional level to the idea of fairness. I had too often seen business terms that implied, essentially, that they were "good enough for *those people*." The practices might have been better than they would have been if impact were not an objective, but they were still fundamentally extractive, rather than reflective of a true acknowledgment of the contributions of all involved.

The principles weren't supposed to be solutions within themselves—we weren't so arrogant as to think we knew all the answers. At the end of the day, our primary objective was to help people focus on the right *questions*, and by doing so enlist the thousands of smart people already working in the field to improve it.

The next step, the group decided, was to create some case studies in alignment with these principles as part of their introduction to help people really get excited about what impact investment could accomplish if it was done more effectively. We wanted to highlight solutions rather than just being naysayers. One of the motivating forces that drove me toward impact investing was being tired of hearing activists talking their heads off about what was wrong with society without offering viable alternatives. We wanted our message to be one-third critique and two-thirds opportunities to do better, so that people would feel like they could be a part of the solution. I began to actively seek out investment projects that followed the principles, and was thrilled to find that there were some great stories to tell and investments to support.

I realized that there was a lot of organizing that needed to be done: of investors, entrepreneurs, and activists—more than I could do myself. We gathered enough interest, both from asset owners and from activists, that I felt we had a mandate to launch a new nonprofit organization, Transform Finance, devoted to creating a community around the principles and putting them to work. I was amazed at the enthusiastic response we received—we were handed our first check literally on the drink line at the SOCAP conference, from David Berge on behalf of the Underdog Foundation (as that we were!).

I wanted to devote my time to investing rather than to organizing at that point in my career, so I recruited my friend and longtime colleague Andrea Armeni to serve as cofounder and executive director. Having started two organizations, one of which had just passed its ten-year anniversary mark, I felt well-situated to mentor someone through that process rather than needing to lead it myself.

The four examples in the next chapters illustrate not only how the Transform Finance principles work in practice, but also how they affect *process*—how the quest for fairness and accountability changed how decisions were made, how structures were established, and how risk and benefit were divided.[*] The interaction of all these elements is what ultimately makes Transform Finance not just a framework but a mindset and a dialogue as well, which hopefully will be implemented and executed in many different ways over the next decade.

Stories about organizations can only capture a moment in time. Depending on when you pick up this book, the organizations I discuss may have completely changed their model, or failed to achieve the impact they desired, or succeeded beyond their wildest dreams. Some have already achieved a great deal; others have not had the opportunity yet to fully actualize their visions. The point of telling these stories is to demonstrate the thinking and process behind various *models* rather than necessarily presenting successful cases; to do the latter would require more time to fairly assess outcomes. If the investment community aligns around the idea that we should take the Transform Finance principles seriously as a component of our work, then ideally more of these projects will have access to the tools and resources they need to grow.

---

*All examples have some connection to Pi Investments or the Libra Foundation as investee or grantee. It seemed prudent to choose the examples that I knew most intimately—as noted throughout the book, examples are provided for purely educational purposes.

six

ENGAGING COMMUNITIES

TRANSFORM FINANCE PRINCIPLE 1:
ENGAGE COMMUNITIES IN DESIGN, GOVERNANCE, AND OWNERSHIP

The key factor that inspired this principle was a desire to be accountable to the communities we serve through effective engagement and shared leadership. Accountability undergirds a basic social justice principle—that of taking guidance from and following the lead of affected communities—as well as the notion that with great power comes great responsibility.

Investors implicitly have power in any interaction. This is not to say that entrepreneurs and communities have no power, but that money gives investors a very specific type of power to make decisions on behalf of others. Those decisions may or may not be informed by a true understanding of the needs, desires, cultures, or values of those on whose behalf they are made.

Every time we negotiate a term sheet, the size of an employee equity pool, the amount of a revenue share to producers, or an interest rate, we make a decision on behalf of an affected community. There are three critical ways we can make sure we stay accountable in the process of such decision-making:

1. Take our social education and connection to affected communities just as seriously as we take our business training.
2. Give it our best effort, even in a world that is too often ready to celebrate "good" before we can identify the "best."
3. Reconsider our design, governance, and ownership structures, to ensure the right people are in a position to make or inform critical decisions in the first place.

SOCIAL EDUCATION AND ACCOUNTABILITY STRUCTURES

The first step in truly engaging communities as an impact investment professional is to take our commitments to impact strategies just as seriously as we take our commitments to investment strategies. As noted in Chapter 3, that means pursuing ongoing education in social and environmental justice issues, cultivating our connections with communities and activists, and developing our expertise in how to have real impact in the process of our impact investing.

For me, that means I can work on valuations and deal terms during the day, and participate in town halls at night as part of my professional commitment. It means that showing up at Facing Race, the nation's largest racial justice conference, is an equally valid use of my time and budget as attending a traditional private equity conference. I have lived for two to three months each year for the past four years in a favela in Brazil, working full-time during the day while spending my nights and weekends more intimately connected with the realities of people earning on average $460 a month, such that our interactions are not so directly mediated by the fact that I am an investor as they would be on a traditional diligence trip.[1] I am also an active musician and dancer, and given the incredible openness of the global arts community, this has provided me with many opportunities to connect deeply with people whose backgrounds may be quite different from mine.

The pathway to connection will be unique for every individual, but it's an important one to explore. Others may not be able to spend as much time as I do traveling or living internationally, but could focus more on connecting across communities at home. They may find ways to connect with people from different class and ethnic backgrounds through sports, spiritual practices, or causes like environmental justice or immigrant rights. My engagement with the arts generally doesn't happen on work time, but I certainly bring this lived experience into my work.

At the end of the day it's *all* part of doing the work. If I stopped any of it I would simply be less effective as an impact investment professional. I should feel free to discuss these efforts in diligence meetings, and I should not hesitate to change my workflow to adapt to what it takes to be connected and informed on both investments *and* impact. That means that sometimes, "dressing professionally" means not wearing a suit, as that would be off-putting to the people with whom I need to build relationships. Sometimes it means intentionally not staying in the fancy hotel in Cape Town or Rio, which would only intensify the differences in both race and class that people may see or feel when they meet me.

It also means adjusting to the fact that for most working-class people, activism happens in the hours of the day that fit with demanding work schedules. It also happens at times when actions are most effective. Just as a West Coast investment banker may need to be up at 6:00 a.m. to be in sync with the New York markets, I needed to be out the door at 6:30 a.m. to support the local Black Lives Matter community in shutting down the Oakland Police Department headquarters, which—and I cannot speak to the exact motivations of the organizers, but I would suspect—had to happen first thing in the morning to be effective as an action.

It may seem like social justice activism and investment work occupy two vastly different worlds, but I find that this kind of engagement is integral to my investment practice and not just about my own personal activism or beliefs. My understanding of how to participate to support racial justice has deepened—and has been greatly informed—by my participation in social movements over the years, even given that my participation has been very limited compared to that of the activists I most admire. I have learned a completely different set of lessons based on experiences interacting with environmental and food justice organizations. I could fill another book with lessons I've learned as an investor on how to evaluate effective entrepreneurs, think about valuations, structure terms, build a balanced portfolio, etc.—the more traditional skill set expected of me. The point is to actively pursue *both* social and financial education as part of embracing the *and* of impact investment.

Mostly, what I've learned from my participation in movements for racial justice is that engaging on race as a white person, and keeping some degree of accountability to communities of color, means understanding what acting in solidarity actually looks and feels like. The Oakland Police Department protest, for example, was explicitly structured for different racial groups to show their solidarity with black people, with very clear roles and responsibilities assigned to each party. It was an incredibly powerful experience to feel the idea of solidarity in action. When people arrived at the protest, a friendly volunteer explained where to stand based on your connection to the issue. Asians for Black Lives were blocking the main door; Black-OUT Collective members were leading the activities from the front of the police headquarters building; and white allies had a designated section in the median across the street. BlackOUT Collective members would yell, "Show us what solidarity looks like!" to the response, "This is what solidarity looks like!"

Even if an ally wanted to be a "leader," as a white or Asian person it simply wasn't one's place to stand at the front of the crowd, push into the press photo, or make decisions. It was pouring rain that day, and while we allies were the least likely to face arrest, we definitely won the competition for being the most freezing and soaking wet. So that's how I showed up to my 10:00 a.m. meeting back at my investment office, to the amusement of my colleagues—"work-appropriate" from my day's activities, and with an important story to tell to that day's set of entrepreneurs.

How do I apply "what solidarity looks like" to impact investment? As someone with both race and class privilege as well as fancy terminology and investor status, I can be at risk of being intimidating, written off as part of "the system," or falsely befriended, depending on who I'm speaking with. So I try to be very conscious of how I present myself when I walk into a room. For example, I often speak very little at first—perhaps for the first hour of any group gathering, and at least until I feel that I have a reasonably good understanding of the power dynamics in play. At that point, or if I'm in more of a convener role, I try to elicit comments from others who are not speaking much, to make sure that those with the loudest voices attend to other types of knowledge and experience among those who are present in the room. And while I may have strong convictions about the power of impact investment, and specific ideas about what exactly it should be, I need to check myself to be especially open-minded when the perspectives of affected communities do not align with my original vision, or someone's exact terminology does not align with the way I am used to hearing things.

I also try to be extra thoughtful about when I know I have power in an interaction, and try to find ways to intentionally cede that power when appropriate. There are times when all of us could better serve social change by staying on the median strip rather than standing on the front line. I make a point of having relationships of accountability with people I trust, who will be honest when I take a wrong turn, when I misstep, or when I misspeak. Feedback is a gift, and I try to have the courage to face my failings when I receive it, rather than collapsing in what antiracist educator Robin DiAngelo astutely calls "white fragility"—which puts the burden on others for the growing pains implicit in raising our individual consciousness.[2]

Why do I try so hard, even when I feel foolish among my peers for doing so? I do it because personal accountability is useful for activists and investors alike. I feel personally compelled to justify the actions that I take as an investor.

People often mention that one of the perks of impact investment is that it gives the traditional financial manager something interesting to talk about at a cocktail party, since unlike simply making more money for wealthy clients, doing something for social benefit will generally be met with a certain amount of admiration. That admiration makes it easy to feel like you're already being accountable and doing something good, especially if your community largely looks and acts like you.

But I want to raise the bar and challenge people to really think about what accountability looks and *feels* like before we pat ourselves on the back for a job well done. I want to be able to look any factory worker or farmer in the eye and say, "Here's how we structured this investment, and why I feel completely comfortable that this was designed to make sure both you and I, and everyone else around the table, was compensated fairly for their work." Some of our investments are structured in a way that forces us as investors, or our entrepreneurs, to actually have to do this on an annual basis, and I am grateful for the opportunity to be kept personally accountable for my definition of impact. I cannot imagine, for instance, going back to a woman in Mexico to say, "I made 250 times my money on the Compartamos IPO, and I'm glad you were able to buy ten chickens."[3] Or, "I am happy you were able to make $6 for this hand-knitted sweater which was just sold at Barney's for $1,200, because they deserve a 70 percent (or higher!) margin." I need to be able to look that person in the eye and have an answer I can justify and be proud of.

This is why, in creating fair systems, it's essential to have structures for accountability that balance the voices around the table in an interaction. If investors and entrepreneurs continue to make decisions in a vacuum without having to justify their actions, their best intentions can easily fall flat. Just trying to do good, without having real connections to relevant social movements to help guide your actions, has the real potential to do more harm than good.

For a vivid example of what can go very right—or extremely wrong—in an impact investment, based on the level of attention paid to community accountability and engagement, let's look at two very different impact project attempts in the indigenous territories of Oaxaca, Mexico. Both examples underscore the importance of Transform Finance Principle 1.

IMPACT INVESTING GONE WRONG

One of the challenges of impact investing is that we are required to know just about everything about everything to do the job right. Which is more environmentally efficient—wind or solar? And what's more effective: household solar or village-level microgrids? Is direct trade better than fair trade? Is a hydroelectric dam a good thing or a bad thing in a particular community?

Get the answer to one of these questions wrong, and you can find yourself very quickly stepping on an impact landmine. I've learned that the best investors don't have to know everything, but they do have to know exactly who to call in each circumstance, and what questions to ask. Even that can be a challenge, as formulating the right questions requires sufficient background knowledge—and we can wind up overly relying on our investment peers, who may or may not have real insight into the on-the-ground dynamics, for information.

In Oaxaca, Mexico, I received a firsthand look at how terribly things can go wrong when impact investors fail to find the right people and ask the right questions. The experience further strengthened my resolve to ensure, no matter how pressed for time we may be in fast-and-furious investment processes, that we're really thoughtful about who to reach out to when assessing projects. We need to do more than just pick up the phone for input from the "usual suspects" of investment insight: we also need to seek out the insights of community-based organizations, social movements, and community members themselves. And as Principle 1 implores, we need to ensure their participation in the design, governance, and ownership of projects from the start. These practices are essential not just to ensure social impact, but also to minimize financial risk, as the following story will illustrate.

Imagine opening your inbox to an impact investor's dream: a series of projects forecasting returns in excess of 20 percent on wind energy in Southern Mexico—the largest wind corridor in Latin America, cofunded by a well-respected development bank, the Mexican government, and a few expert wind companies. The wind companies have signed agreements with the local indigenous authorities, getting the green light to install the turbines. They intend to supply the country with a renewable resource to offset over a million tons of carbon while creating hundreds of jobs in poor communities. The amount to be invested is $550 million, and the development bank has done its impact due diligence and approved the project.

What's not to like?

As the Mexican press and numerous community organizations have reported, plenty. When this project came together in 2012, its decision-makers failed to recognize the depth of community opposition. Here's what one local observer had to say about it, as reported in *Renewable Energy Mexico*: "The creation of the wind corridor in the Isthmus of Tehuantepec, developed mainly by Spanish firms, has almost become the new conquest because the indigenous Zapoteco and Ikoot communities have been basically evicted from 12 thousand hectares through unfair and disadvantageous contracts, in order to generate electric energy with their wind and on their land, in the benefit of private initiative."[4]

It turned out that land had been taken from communities often for as little as $50 per month in "rent." If that wasn't bad enough, it was done in an aggressive and violent manner, including through unlawful detention and infliction of physical harm against local protesters who spoke out against the project. On November 5, 2012, the Assembly of Indigenous Peoples of the Isthmus of Tehuantepec in Defense of Land and Territory reported that authorities had "fired bullets and discharged pepper spray at women, youth and old people, beating several of those present, including pregnant women. The police detained 9 people, among these 2 women, without giving any information about the charges or where the prisoners would be taken." The Assembly of Indigenous Peoples then issued a statement against the project:

No windpower project on the Tehuantepec Isthmus. . . .
    Stop the intimidation, hostility and violence generated by the windpower project.[5]

Yes, you read that right. The intimidation, hostility, and violence were caused not by terrorists, not by oil companies, but by . . . *wind energy companies*? And the project was being

funded not just by evil greedy banks, but by . . . impact investors and development banks, too?

How in the world did this happen?

In short, it happened because foreign companies developed
projects without thinking through their community engagement strategies or making any attempt to share financial returns fairly. In this instance, the concept of "social impact"
was undermined and distorted. Investors were likely told that
they were going to be a major force in spreading renewable energy in Latin America—a seemingly great impact story—but
they fell into the trap of letting impact be defined solely by
investors and entrepreneurs, without consulting the supposed
beneficiaries.

I had the opportunity to visit these communities in 2014,
alongside Andrea Armeni, the executive director of Transform
Finance, and our exceptionally knowledgeable and dedicated
tour guide, Sergio Oceransky, the founder of Grupo Yansa.
Here are some stories we heard in our first twenty-four hours
on the ground that got missed in the diligence process conducted by the development banks. Note that these stories in-
volve various wind-farm investment projects over a period of
five years, all in the same region as the project noted above.
Also note that in most cases the stories demonstrate that
the "agreements" with indigenous communities were poorly
crafted, or, in some cases, downright illegal.

» In one village, the signed agreements covered and were
   supposed to compensate the village only for exploration
   of the land's potential. But the companies involved went
   ahead and installed the turbines without getting a second
   agreement allowing them to actually use the land. Only

after the turbines were a fait accompli did the companies offer the village the ridiculous sum of 50 pesos (about $3 at the time) a year for each one. The result was a protracted legal battle that may end with local villagers possessing both the turbines and the substation—a potential loss of millions to investors.

» In another village, when the local government "accepted" the wind company's terms (after, it is suspected, the company gave sizable kickbacks to corrupt officials), community members stormed the municipal government building and took it over in protest. While the occupiers could certainly have been a radical few, when elections came up a few months later, the community democratically voted for these "occupiers" to become the official local government and to fight back to cancel the wind agreements. Popular opinion clearly was not on the side of the wind project, and in this case for a relatively straightforward reason that the wind company might have addressed had it done the necessary outreach: the noise the turbines produced had been historically known to drive away the shrimp population, which is what this fishing community depended upon for its survival.

» There is now an open case with the UN Permanent Forum on Indigenous Issues against the Mexican government for approving certain projects. The Mexican government officials wrote a letter back to the United Nations explaining that they had followed standards for "free prior informed consent," also known as FPIC, by posting plans on a website for a ten-day open comment period. A fisherman explained this to me, his voice dripping with irony, as we sat in the dark in his village's town hall—where there is barely phone service and electricity, let alone widespread Internet access.

How did investors get these projects in the Isthmus of Tehuantepec so terribly, terribly wrong?

There are some theories—mainly that the development bank felt the need to make a major announcement of some progress on renewable energy before the Conference of the Parties (COP13) of the Convention on Biological Diversity, a major climate change summit, and that other investors just followed along after the development bank committed. But whether a mistake like this is made in Oaxaca or Kenya— where there is a similarly famous case near Lake Turkana— the renewable energy sector and impact investors are likely to wind up inducing some serious unintended consequences if they don't stay on top of land-grab issues that community organizations around the world have been fighting over the past few decades. Our ignorance could lead to more poor impact choices—and major regrets when we not only wind up on the wrong side of history, but potentially lose our money as well.

But if we make thoughtful decisions about who to talk to (that is, if we talk to local community organizations, not just financiers), and about what questions to ask (How were communities engaged in design, governance, and ownership? What percentage of project revenue will stay in the community? As the Rotary Club would ask, does the deal feel *fair to all*?), we can ensure that our impact is positive, deep, and long-lasting. We won't always get it perfect—far from it—but if we are more careful to take our marching orders from affected communities themselves, we are much less likely to have our good intentions backfire. And that's exactly what Grupo Yansa has done.

IMPACT INVESTING DONE RIGHT

In reaction to the trend of destructive development, community members on the Isthmus of Tehuantepec declared that they were not against wind energy per se, but against corporate control of their lands. They began to consider ways in which they could implement wind energy on their own lands on their own terms. Working with Grupo Yansa, they have come up with a model for community-owned wind intended to deliver strong returns to investors while equally benefiting the local community. The project plan explained below was approved in the pueblo's general assembly, its forum for group decision-making.

Grupo Yansa's pilot project was developed in the indigenous Zapotec pueblo of Ixtepec, a large community with over 30,000 inhabitants that is endowed with a very rich wind resource—making the town in general a very pleasant, breezy place. The community maintains common ownership and management over their land and resources, an arrangement dating back for centuries and codified into law after the Mexican Revolution of 1910–1920. This communal-property status makes it difficult for the community to use its land as collateral. It is therefore very challenging for the community to obtain the amount of financing required to develop a wind farm.

However, Mexico's state-owned electrical utility offers twenty-year contracts to energy producers that lock in production at a fixed price. So long as the community can secure the contract (and, of course, execute on energy production), it is guaranteed income for the energy it produces, significantly reducing risk to investors. A debt structure for external investors would ensure community ownership of the project, as the community would retain the equity.

The profit that remains each year would be divided on a 50–50 basis between Grupo Yansa and the community. The 50 percent of profits going to the community would be administered by a community trust devoted to strengthening quality of life, economic opportunities, and environmental sustainability, with an elected board overseeing expenditures, per village custom. For instance, community members proposed the idea of creating pension funds for elders—a way to prevent young people from having to migrate, as their elders will be less dependent on remittances—a benefit that could be equally shared by community members, as everyone will eventually be eligible.

The 50 percent of profits going to Yansa would be used to finance more community-owned renewable energy projects. Renewable energy projects would therefore finance a broad framework of integral and sustainable community development that is partly based on solidarity and sharing between different communities. Yansa's financial participation in future projects would serve as a guarantee layer, giving Yansa access to a wider range of institutional investors who are interested in safe returns and high social and environmental impact.

Globally, thousands of communities are deeply concerned about "land grabs" in the name of clean energy. But regardless of the industry, and whether it's land rights or labor treatment or the preservation of the environment that is at stake, some basic questions must be considered in any impact investment:

What is our responsibility as impact investors to make sure we are accountable to the communities in which we work? How do we, like Grupo Yansa, find ways to put communities front and center in the design, governance, and ownership of projects? And, as investors, how do we avoid the financial risk that comes from disregarding community will? What can we do to keep the brand of "intimidation, hostility and violence" far away from us?

The point is not that all projects should adopt Grupo Yansa's model—but rather to learn from the way this group has effectively made community accountability through effective design, governance, and ownership models a pillar of its work, to the benefit of both communities and investors.

seven

ADDING MORE VALUE THAN YOU EXTRACT

TRANSFORM FINANCE PRINCIPLE 2:
ADD MORE VALUE THAN YOU EXTRACT

It's Buenos Aires, 2001. Imagine that you're a factory owner and you have done quite well for yourself. You keep a couple of bank accounts in both Argentinian pesos and US dollars for security. But as Argentina begins to suffer from the tremendous recession spreading throughout the world, rumors surface that the government is going to prevent all bank withdrawals and convert all dollars to pesos—right before depegging the peso to the dollar, sending the value of those dollars plummeting to a fraction of their current worth. What do you do?

If you're like most factory owners of the day, you make a run at the bank, grab your cash, take anything else that can fit on your back, and run over the border to Brazil, Uruguay, or just about anywhere else but Argentina.

Anyone who didn't adopt this strategy quickly enough had their wealth reduced by close to 75 percent as the exchange rate slid from 1.4 to 4 pesos to the dollar.[1] The result was that literally tens of thousands of factory workers showed up to their jobs to find the boss gone, his keys on the desk, with last month's (and next month's) wages somewhere outside the country.

But, sitting on piles of lemons—the abandoned factories, still equipped with whatever machinery was too heavy for the owners to carry—the workers literally made, and sold, lemonade. Thousands of workers joined forces to take over their factories and get to work as cooperatively owned and managed enterprises. The police spent months trying to kick them out—a struggle well documented in Avi Lewis and Naomi Klein's documentary *The Take*. But as the workers kept returning to work after each attempted eviction, the government ultimately realized that with a 25 percent unemployment rate, and more than 40,000 individuals trying to make their living collecting cardboard boxes to sell for recycling, they could do worse than to have workers self-organize and take advantage of these stranded assets. So they ultimately let the workers stay.[2]

Brendan Martin was one of many Americans who went to Argentina at this time to learn from, and work in solidarity with, this new movement of more than two hundred worker-owned cooperatives.[3] Outside of Mondragon in Spain, a town famously run by a community of cooperatives, it was rare to see cooperatives in action on such a significant scale in one place, and the phenomenon attracted many who dreamed of creating a more co-op-driven economy. Brendan saw quickly that lack of capital was a huge challenge for these new co-ops. Availability of capital for small enterprises was, and is, severely restricted, and Argentina's mainstream banking sector had little or no reach into the poorer sections of the country's economy—especially in the middle of a crisis. Furthermore, traditional microcredit programs were limited to individuals and small-scale cottage industries, and they frequently encouraged debt-funded consumption rather than real asset creation. Thus, large sectors of Argentina's working poor, including the newly formed cooperatives, were left without access to capital or business training.

In response to these needs, Brendan founded The Working World (TWW, or in Spanish, La Base), a technical assistance and social investment organization specifically designed for the unique needs of worker-owned cooperatives. The organization focused not only on capital provision but also on sharing best practices in collective decision-making and management processes with these relatively new organizations.[4] Since its inception in 2004, it has provided more than 1,000 investments to 103 cooperatives in Argentina—disbursing a total of over $4.5 million—with a record of full repayment for 98 percent of the loans. TWW has also expanded to Nicaragua and the United States with an additional $5 million (and growing) fund—and has shown time after time how worker co-ops can revive failing economies with long-term, systemic solutions. Investors in The Working World include individuals, foundations, and, increasingly, the co-ops themselves, whose members seek to support their peers.

Financing worker-owned co-ops by any means inherently increases assets for the working class, as they become owners of the means of production. Brendan's primary innovation was in response to the question of what type of capital is actually appropriate to best grow the assets of working people. His solution, nonextractive finance, has implications not just for worker-owned cooperatives, and for his relatively small fund, but for the economy as a whole.

Brendan's "light-bulb" moment came during a visit to a textile company in Buenos Aires, early in the life of The Working World. While walking through the very active factory, he was surprised to see a relatively new piece of machinery sitting idle. He asked the workers why this was so. "That machine?" one responded. "That's the one the microfinance bank encouraged us to buy. It turned out to not actually be useful, but we still pay the monthly payments."

It upset Brendan to see hard-working people having to turn over their earnings to pay for an unproductive asset. A loan is supposed to be an input that enhances profitability, not detract from it. Why should the co-op take full responsibility for the bad advice of a financier? In that moment he committed to the idea that TWW's investments had to add more value than they extracted; otherwise, he could not claim to be "helping" the poor, and might as well pack up and go home.

For the most part, The Working World's daily work looks like that of any credit provider. It offers small amounts of capital to worker-owned cooperatives in order to help them expand their ventures. Cooperatives first receive several small short-term investments to test the relationship, and as trust is established, they may access larger amounts of capital for longer terms. For each investment, TWW staff members work with the cooperative to create an accompanying detailed business plan and timeline. The business plan must be approved by the membership of the cooperative alongside TWW. The Working

World's loan officers carefully and consistently monitor the business plan and investment repayment, visiting the project weekly to check in on progress and give feedback and support. At each stage, the organization seeks to empower workers with financial literacy, business planning, and management skills to ensure the long-term success of the operation.

Where TWW's processes differ from those of most investors is in how it structures deals. Deals are designed to achieve two key objectives: to help grow wealth for the cooperative members receiving the investment, and to lower risk in order to protect the fund for future projects within the larger community. Each deal therefore must fit the following three criteria:[5]

1. *Repayments must be drawn exclusively from the productive outputs of the investment made:* If the investment isn't effective, in that it doesn't serve to help increase the cooperative's profitability, the cooperative isn't responsible to pay it back. This provision shifts the primary risk to The Working World, giving Brendan and his team a strong incentive to ensure that the recipients develop sound business plans and use the investments for their intended purposes. It also ensures that no project will create unforeseen hardship for the group it is intended to help. In other words, if The Working World advises a factory to buy a machine that turns out to be a dud, The Working World is equally responsible, and can't just push all the risk onto the workers. Likewise, if the investment is smart and strategic, The Working World will rightfully benefit alongside the co-op, as the deal is structured to provide for revenue sharing alongside

a base interest rate, giving it more upside potential than the typical debt fund.

2. *Any investment received by the fund must yield a higher return for the target community than it does for the investor:* Workers receive the majority of the benefit, as it's the sweat and tears of the co-op members leveraging the investor's capital that ultimately create the value. Like any tool, capital is useless unless human hands pick it up and build something with it.

   This does not prohibit the investor from making a return, and potentially even a "market-rate" one, depending on the overall level of profitability of the enterprise. But the assumption is that labor ultimately worked harder than capital—and each should be paid proportionate to its efforts.

   This criterion greatly raises the incentive for the cooperative members to give it their all, since they know that they truly stand to benefit the most from any successful initiative. Intimately tying investor and worker success, while ultimately prioritizing the asset accumulation of workers, serves to both motivate the workers and ensure their fair treatment while still ensuring that investors benefit from enhanced profitability. In short, it creates a more win-win scenario than one where workers fear their hard efforts are largely accruing returns for outside investors—a very demotivating concept indeed.

3. *There must be a no-tolerance policy for laziness:* The cooperative must make a good-faith effort to execute the plan specified by the project, or it can become responsible for repayment with assets outside of the

project. This condition is stated explicitly in the contract, and while it's ultimately the call of the loan officer, it's usually quite clear to all involved if insufficient "sweat equity" is being put in by the co-op members. Investments are typically used to buy assets that can be easily liquidated, such that if liquidation becomes necessary due to a lack of effort (or just genuine business failure), as much capital as possible can be recouped to loan to the next co-op.

Skeptics might say this model is ripe for moral hazard: Why try to succeed if you know you don't have to pay back if you fail? But that argument ignores the inherent vulnerability of working people. In many working-class communities, failure doesn't mean you pack up, declare bankruptcy, and try the next idea; it means your children may not eat that night. That's a pretty strong incentive to do your best—more of an incentive, I would posit, than the one spurring on an Ivy League graduate who has the safety net of numerous job opportunities if his startup fails. If you know, as owner, that you stand to be the primary beneficiary of your work, above and beyond the external financier, then you will do everything possible to keep the doors open and enhance profitability. Having The Working World as a flexible financing partner—somewhere in between equity and debt—aligns incentives, as truly everyone wins when a co-op succeeds and its members are motivated to work hard toward mutually developed goals.

Brendan recognized that his work in Buenos Aires took place in the context of a very specific moment and social movement. To prove that his model worked, and that nonextractive finance could be a scalable tool for communities and investors, he thought he should also demonstrate its effectiveness in the birth country of modern finance—the United States. And there he found that, by using the nonextractive methodology, and incentivizing workers through the opportunity of ownership, he could once again make gold out of the dust created by the traditional financial system.

In Chicago, the workers of Republic Windows and Doors were tired of each new factory owner threatening to lay them all off—not because the factory itself was unprofitable, but because the other business interests of the owner were interfering with the destiny of the factory. When the factory came up for sale—its most recent owner actually winding up in jail—seventeen workers, all people of color, came together to buy it as New Era, a cooperative, with financing support from The Working World. The proud new owners are putting in more hours than ever before, but now they know, given TWW's financing structures, that they will be the primary beneficiaries of all their hard work. So far, they have made all of their required payments, and they are working their way toward profitability as the only minority-owned manufacturing facility in the state of Illinois.

Republic Windows and Doors is now just one of more than twenty-five worker-owned cooperatives that TWW has financed in the United States over the past three years,[6] without any losses to date. In the process, Brendan and his colleagues are slowly but surely proving that you can make money for investors at a rate comparable to other impact private-debt funds—while still ensuring that investors add more value than they extract. When investments like this work—and prove both stable and profitable—it paves the way for deep structural change to the economy.

eight

BALANCING RISK AND RETURN

TRANSFORM FINANCE PRINCIPLE 3:
FAIRLY BALANCE RISK AND RETURN BETWEEN
INVESTORS, ENTREPRENEURS, AND COMMUNITIES

Typically, social businesses with limited access to capital are at the mercy of investors to set the structure of a deal, in terms of both how much risk each party will take on and how much each party will potentially benefit.

Investors, logically, often do all they can to protect their own interests. At times, they also take advantage of this unequal power relationship. For instance, major banks will sometimes make an enterprise somehow obtain a 100 percent guarantee for their loan, ensuring zero losses and requiring other actors, such as MicroCredit Enterprises or Shared Interest, to step in and pick up the slack. Other investors will at times require a company to reimburse them for the time they spend learning about the company, a process called due diligence. Such policies enable them to diminish their risk substantially while still having full access to the anticipated investment returns.

Now, think for a moment about the entrepreneur, and his or her team, who—depending on the country and context—may be making just the bare minimum to survive. If the enterprise fails, the bank has its 100 percent guarantee to make it whole. But all these people, who put in years of sweat: What is their return? Not only do they completely lose any resources they may have put in, but they also now have to find a new livelihood.

These are the concerns behind Transform Finance Principle 3. Behind the idea of balancing risk and return is the idea that we owe it to the communities we work with to do the best we can to be fair to all parties. Even if we have the power to demand terms that put all the risk on the enterprise, we can choose, in alignment with our overall intention of maximizing value creation for the communities we serve, even as we create value for ourselves, to focus on creating terms that more fairly share risk and return. One way to frame this principle as social investors is to ask ourselves who we should try harder to protect from risk: the people with wealth, or the people without?

This chapter tells a story about a company that committed deeply to doing what is fair in an industry that had stopped short at what was deemed to be better—the cacao industry. Not only are the company's internal practices extremely thoughtful with regard to how to share risk and return between the enterprise and the farmers they work with, but it also worked to figure out an investment structure that would reflect these values and more fairly distribute risk and return to all parties.

The logic of capitalism is leading chocolate down the road to extinction. Cacao farmers, who often make the equivalent of as little as 50 cents a day globally, are giving up and getting out.[1] Their abandonment of the cacao crop has global chocolate makers like Mars deeply worried—alongside concerned consumers, some of whom see chocolate as a basic necessity alongside air and water.

Efforts to secure farmers more money and a better standard of living in exchange for their labor—notably, through the fair trade certification system—have certainly helped, but they have not solved the problem. That failure is in part a byproduct of the methodology by which fair trade works.

The modern-day fair trade labeling system was launched in 1988, primarily to remove the volatility in commodity pricing for agricultural products such as coffee, cacao, and bananas and to establish floor prices that would keep growers out of destitute poverty. Rather than having to accept the market price with its highs and lows, fair trade producers would be guaranteed a basic minimum, and then, if the world commodity price got above that minimum, they would always get an additional small markup (traditionally 3 cents a kilo for coffee, for instance) above the commodity price. In addition, a "fair trade premium" is paid to agricultural co-ops, rather than to each farmer directly, to help to pay for initiatives requiring collective action, such as building an irrigation system for a village.[2]

This system certainly has helped provide some stability to farmers, but it has had some major drawbacks. Fair trade pricing isn't high enough to enable farmers to actually rise out of poverty, and it doesn't establish fairness across the supply chain. As the world price for cacao and other commodities has increased over the past decade, in part due to the fear of shortages, a few cents a kilo of benefit can feel pretty miserly, especially when products labeled "fair trade" can command much higher prices in the market, to the benefit of manufacturers and retailers, that farmers will never see. Even fair trade co-ops, like any other political institution, are not immune to corruption. Some cooperatives are great at democratic process, have strong leadership, and use fair trade premiums to carry out fantastic local projects. Others are highly corrupt, such that premiums designed to serve the community instead serve only a privileged few.

Quality has also suffered in the fair trade system. Because the fair trade label is quality-agnostic, farmers have an incentive essentially to "dump" the worst-quality product onto the fair trade system, knowing they will get the same price no matter what, whereas their higher-quality product might be able to fetch a higher price elsewhere with or without the fair trade marker. There has been little attention to processing improvements for cacao co-ops that struggle to maintain quality, particularly when growing organically. As the chocolate buyer and consultant Chloé Doutre-Roussel wrote in her book *The Chocolate Connoisseur*, "Every time I eat organic chocolate a little voice in my head says: Just let me give a cheque to the co-operative, but please don't make me eat this!"[3]

Partly as a result of the skewed incentives that led to product quality erosion in the fair trade system, the "direct trade" movement arose. Coffee purchasers who wanted to pick and choose among producers based on quality would then typically pay a significantly higher price than even fair trade offered, and tell that story to consumers through laminated signs and happy photos in their shops. However, these negotiations and transactions took place as one-off deals with no outside certification or minimum requirements, so even if the results were perhaps better for farmers in the short term, direct trade lacked the long-term impact and accountability structures that the fair trade system intended to provide.

FAIRER THAN FAIR?

So how could one marry the best aspects of fair trade and direct trade—establish a consistent metric for a "living wage" price, incentivize quality production, and provide some collective resources to pay for community-level needs—all with transparency and accountability?

Emily Stone found herself in Belize in 2010 trying to solve this exact quandary. A native Bostonian, she had been sent on a fact-finding mission by the founder of Taza, a local company that was a pioneer in the "bean to bar" movement in chocolate. Taza's founder had heard that cacao in Belize had previously been highly regarded, but that quality had declined over the past decade. Could an origin-focused chocolate company help revive the sector before families abandoned the crop—and hundreds of years of agricultural culture and tradition—for other, more profitable pursuits?[4]

Belize is a tiny country, with just over 360,000 people. It has one of the most diverse populations in Latin America: a mix of Q'eq'chi- and Mopan-speaking indigenous people; Garifuna-speaking people of African origin; and mestizo Spanish-speaking people, although the official language is English. Given its thriving tourism industry, average per capita annual income in Belize is estimated to be approximately $8,600, among the highest in Latin America—but the average farmer was getting by on just US$200 a month.[5]

In the south of Belize, cacao production was largely organized by the Toledo Cacao Growers Association—a fair trade association that farmers were slowly but surely abandoning. Visitors driving on the highway into Punta Gorda would pass by the half-constructed Museum of Cacao—a $500,000 project designed by the association, paid for with fair trade premiums, to grow tourism in the region. The museum was becoming overgrown by Belize's lush vegetation and threatening to disappear into the forest before hosting a single visitor.

The farmers continued to sell cacao onto the world market. Despite functioning administratively as a cooperative, they processed their cacao individually—each farmer removing the pulp, drying the beans, and fermenting them. The fermenting process, when the character of the beans emerges, is, along with the plant's origin, or *terroir*, the greatest determinant of flavor, and thus a critical part of the process. And like all things in life that require some skill and knowledge, some farmers were better at fermentation than others, leading to major quality variations. Given the uneven nature of fermentation across so many small farms, it was hard for the farmers to collectively maintain high quality and thus fetch the best price—so they continued along earning the historically low commodity price for cacao, plus an additional premium under the fair trade system.

Emily knew next to nothing about cacao at this point, but as a former member of Green Corps—a training program for organizers in the environmental movement—she knew how to connect with a community. She literally went door to door to the homes at over a hundred farms asking about cacao production and what it would take to build a more robust sector, preparing to "lead from behind" in response to community needs.

On one of those door-knocking expeditions she met Gabriel Pop, whose family had been farming cacao for generations. He was frustrated by the fair trade system and had also been looking for ways to make cacao a more sustainable enterprise for his family and community.

Gabriel agreed to partner with Emily, backed by Taza and others, to create a new company called Maya Mountain Cacao. He was unpaid at first, by his own choice, as he wanted to make sure their values were aligned and that she was fully committed to the community before agreeing to accept any compensation. Five years later, they had built the largest exporter of cacao from Belize. Maya Mountain Cacao is now one of several companies that sell together under the brand of Uncommon Cacao—which has become a global cacao sourcing company that focuses on quality, transparency, and a pathway out of poverty for farmers.

The secret sauce of Maya Mountain Cacao was its laser focus on improving quality, which it saw as the best pathway to improved pricing for farmers. Most agricultural interventions focus on having farmers do more processing themselves, thereby taking a greater role in the "value-added" part of the agricultural supply chain, which in theory would allow them to make more money. The company's key insight was that by centralizing drying and fermentation, they could significantly enhance quality, and thus create a truly unique product that chocolate makers would fight for—and pay a lot more for.

The strategy worked—ironically—by taking some processing out of the farmers' hands. Centralization not only gave many farmers more time in the day to invest as they pleased, but also gave them three times as much income. In 2015, Belize's beans were nominated to become a World Heritage product, and they fetched among the highest prices of any on the market. In fact, in a 2014 Kickstarter campaign, chocolatiers paid $86,721 not for Maya Mountain Cacao beans, but just for the *right* to buy those rare and precious beans, at whatever price, at some point in the future.[6]

Recognizing the global trend toward higher-quality chocolate, a trend similar to the one that saw specialty coffee consumption go from 3 percent to 51 percent of market value over a twenty-year period, Emily, alongside her cofounders from Taza and Belize, saw an opportunity to replicate this formula of improving quality and providing higher prices to farmers throughout the world.[7]

They also knew that farmers, who were used to getting a bad deal for their product, would be thrilled with any additional benefit the company could provide—the classic stopping point for social enterprises. But in alignment with their social mission and the core values of the company, and in order to guarantee transparency and dignity for all, they felt they owed farmers more. This wasn't just about their social mission; it was also a savvy business practice, since ensuring that all stakeholders would benefit from the company's success was a way to build loyalty and encourage hard work.

From their humble start in Belize, the founders had a vision of a global company with a balanced stakeholder table—farmers, employees, owners, investors, and chocolatiers all united in the same purpose. To achieve this vision it was important to design pricing, investment, and ownership structures that balanced risk and return across the board.

BALANCING RISK AND RETURN

Maya Mountain Cacao raised its first round of capital in 2014—a process I supported through my work at Pi Investments, precisely because we knew we had aligned interests in pushing supply chains to maximize benefit for all.

Knowing our expertise in community ownership models and transformative finance, Emily asked us to help facilitate a conversation among the Maya Mountain Cacao team on these themes in Belize. At that point, the company in Belize, led by Emily and Gabriel, had three key employees, Anna, Deon, and Maya (Maya would eventually lead the US-based sourcing business for Uncommon Cacao), and they worked alongside a few hundred farmers. The company was in the process of starting to work in Guatemala as well, and was beginning to think more about what governance and ownership, and distribution of benefit, would look like over the long term as it went global.

The team invited me to join them in Belize to lead a summit around the concepts of governance and ownership. Over five very long days we went through intensive exercises to try to answer questions such as, What should the ideal division of equity be? What are the major decisions the company will face—and who should be empowered to make them?

We left this meeting with an eight-page manifesto describing ownership percentages, an intensive committee structure for collective governance purposes, and profit-sharing structures. It was far too complex to imagine implementing exactly as written. But it was a great distillation of what multiple parties—founders, investors, employees, and farmers—felt about how the company should grow in a way that could provide fair benefit to all parties involved.

When it then came time for the company's Series A—the next major investment round to help the company grow—Pi Investments facilitated a lead investment in the company, meaning we helped set the investment terms and worked to inspire others to join. A lead investor can make or break a round; if the lead negotiates poor terms or is perceived negatively in the field, it can make it very hard to raise capital. So we took this responsibility seriously and dug in to complete the three parts of our process: financial diligence, impact diligence, and the negotiation of terms.

The impact diligence actually took some time and conversation, and it allowed for the company to solidify its core practices. We worked with company management to develop a simple, one-page statement of impact that would define standards addressing how risk and benefit would be divided among the parties. Ultimately, when negotiating terms, we agreed that investors could ask the company to collect broad stakeholder input before any substantial alterations to those standards were made. The box on the next page shows the simple text we put together to articulate the social commitment.

We addressed the division of risk and return in finer detail when we established the investment terms, which set the valuation of the company, the ownership percentages, and the right to make certain key decisions.

The National Venture Capital Alliance has issued a set of "standard" documents that tend to be used over and over again in making deals. The thinking is that these standards do a good job of protecting investors, and that it therefore makes sense not to reinvent the wheel on each investment deal. We didn't want to reinvent the wheel, but we did want

When farmers and chocolate makers work with Uncommon Cacao Source + Trade, they're signing up for a better supply chain. Globally, the vast majority of the world's 5 million cacao farming families live in destitute poverty despite supplying a fast-growing and high-value market. The failure to pay farmers better prices for cacao is causing widespread abandonment of cacao plots as farmers age and their children choose other crops or careers. Traditional certifications like Fair Trade attach premiums to the price dictated by the volatile commodities market. For farmers at origin, certification requires being part of a cooperative and can cost more for the cooperative than the income received through the premium, which rarely trickles down to farmers' pockets; and for chocolate makers, the certification does not assure delivery of quality cacao. At Uncommon Cacao, we know that the best way to generate impact is by focusing on fair pay for great quality. To put it simply, we put more money in farmers' pockets, by reliably supplying chocolate makers with the fine flavor cacao they need.

At Uncommon Cacao we guarantee a price floor to farmer groups, with price incentives tied to clear quality standards. Our goal is for cacao farmers to finally receive a living income for their work. We work directly with chocolate makers to get the best and most stable price possible for the farmers in our supply chain. To ensure that farmers are benefitting from their hard work, we have a 49% gross margin cap on our business. Uncommon Cacao contributes any annual gross profit beyond that to a Farmer Fund, which is open for technical assistance project applications from all cacao farmer groups working with Uncommon Cacao, and governed by farmers and supply chain experts. We also share 10% of our annual net profit as a business with the Farmer Fund, ensuring farmers benefit as we grow our business alongside and with them.

—continues—

—continued—

Uncommon Cacao offers a supply chain based on authenticity and mutual respect. We empower farmers by openly sharing where value exchanges hands. Our supply chain delivers higher value to farmers and farmer organizations that work with us, and our commitment to radical transparency sets a new industry standard, which we believe will catalyze industry-shifting change for all cacao farmers globally by exposing the low pay for farmers and giving chocolate makers and consumers access to information for more informed buying decisions.

to make sure the deal we constructed was fair, not just to protect the investors, but the farmers and employees, too. So we went through a somewhat unusual process of thinking about the division of risk and return to respective stakeholders—farmers, employees, investors, and founders. What was each being required to contribute, and were they getting fairly compensated for their risk? Was each "standard" clause fair to all parties—or did some need to be redefined through this lens of fairness?

What we discovered by doing this exercise is that, by accepting standard terms, investors often make implicit assumptions about risk and reward. For instance, employee equity pools typically are expected to come out of the founder's shares—meaning the founder takes on the full burden. Given how much we value and encourage employee ownership—not just because of our desire for fairness, but because it motivates people to do their best work—we thought: Shouldn't we as investors contribute to the employee pool, too?

With these new standards in mind, we developed a document laying out the terms of relative risk and reward that later informed the ultimate allocation of ownership in the company (see box).

RISK/REWARD ANALYSIS: UNCOMMON CACAO

Founders retain a majority stake in the company for ease of governance and assurance that the vision be maintained; and we all feel they are sufficiently motivated by the mission and collective values of all stakeholders to represent everyone's interests well. Their shares have already vested as they have proven as a team that they have, and will continue to add, tremendous value. Except for the CEO, they are not compensated, and thus from a liquidity perspective come after investors, as they share the risk, and additionally have contributed significant capital over time.

Investors primarily contribute capital; hence, their ownership stake is very simply based on the amount of money they put in, at what we agreed was a reasonable valuation. While founders, employees, and farmers have to produce quality work to "earn their keep," and/or already had a vesting period, investors put in 100% of their capital upfront and thus have already fulfilled their commitment.

They have some decision-making rights to protect their capital, but not *too* much such that they'd get in the way of day to day decision-making by better equipped founders and employees and farmers.

Employees sit in the middle on the risk-reward continuum. They are provided with living wages (or better) on an annual basis, so unlike the founders or investors receive most of their benefit up front.

—continues—

—*continued*—

However, acknowledging that they deserve to participate in value that is created, and since as rational human beings they may be additionally motivated to make better long-term decisions if they are thinking about long-term value creation, they have the ability to participate in the equity pool.

Farmers are by nature the primary beneficiary of all company activities. They are first in line to receive payment at a living wage standard, and given the 49% margin cap receive the majority of revenue on an absolute basis. If the company grows as anticipated, their 10% annual profit share via the Farmer's Fund could be substantial. Farmers also care more about cash in hand on a year to year basis, and are potentially more transient than employees, so having their profit participation be annual makes more sense than having it all come at the end.

If there is a liquidity event, however, it does make sense that farmers would participate to some extent in that event alongside other stakeholders, since they were a major part of building the company. But because their profit share comes before any employee profit share via dividends, it makes sense for the Farmer's Fund to have less equity than employees.*

*This analysis was initially an internal document and was created not to make a statement for the outside world, but rather to clarify the understanding among the key parties in the deal concerning risk and reward in the enterprise. It is shared here with the company's permission.

I should note that the company's main values are transparency and quality. The story I am telling now is, ironically, not even central to their day-to-day impact thesis, but rather a by-product of the founding team's determination to support the community on its own terms. For them, inclusive process and fairness had to be an undercurrent of all that happened in the company, rather than merely virtues to leverage for a PR headline.

At the end of the day, the effort to balance risk and return between investors, entrepreneurs, employees, and communities served to strengthen the respect and trust between these groups, which in turn fostered the transparency, quality, and commitment that they sought. Time will tell if they equally serve the objectives of greater profitability and impact outcomes for all parties.

nine

MAXIMIZING IMPACT

OUR PURPOSE WITH THE TRANSFORM FINANCE PRINCIPLES was to focus in on a framework for defining and strengthening impact, one embodied by the last few stories. The next question becomes: Even if our intentions and underlying structures are good, how can we ensure we're actually having the impact we desire?

In the early days of the impact investment industry, impact measurement was a hot topic. The first effort to standardize impact measurement, called IRIS, the Impact Reporting and Investment Standards, was created with support from the Rockefeller Foundation.[1] IRIS is essentially a taxonomy that helps to define key terms—for instance, what is the difference between a part-time job and a full-time job?—and lets investment funds choose their own indicators and goals from an extensive list that can be accessed for free online. Later, GIIRS, the Global Impact Investment Rating System, was designed as a more specific survey to help companies assess their overall social and environmental impact, and provided an easy-to-read dashboard that could be compared across companies or a portfolio.[2]

IRIS and GIIRS were (and continue to be) critical pieces of movement infrastructure, as they ensured that funds and enterprises could make apples to apples comparisons about impact. While these systems were great at *measuring* impact, they were not explicitly designed as tools to help people *manage* for impact and ensure it would be enhanced over time. There is a business adage that says, "What gets measured, gets managed"—but achieving the ultimate goal, of course, requires knowing how to manage, not just how to measure.

Here's what financial management looks like: companies typically create quarterly financial statements and cash flow projections for the use of their management team and investors. The management team then will conduct analysis centered around questions about how they are performing compared to their projections; what practices have led to greater effectiveness; what tweaks need to be made to enhance performance; and the like. Moving forward, these questions then help shape the next quarter's activities, which will again be accounted for in the next review. Depending on subsequent performance, management team members may be rewarded or let go.

Now imagine if a company only produced a financial report at the end of the year that said, "This year, we made x amount of money and we spent y amount of money. We have no goals for the upcoming year, and our compensation will not be affected by what we achieve or don't achieve. We will provide our next report in twelve months."

Yes, that is some form of measurement, but it's definitely not management. And yet it's exactly the type of reporting that guided many first-generation impact investment funds. Often, reporting consisted of indicators as simple as how many people were served, how many were women, and how much money was invested—without any color on how deeply interventions helped shift lives, and without going so far as to propose strategies to enhance impact in the future.

These days, we are paying more attention to active *impact management*—yes, our investment had *x* verifiable impact today, but how do we ensure that impact is *x plus 1*, if not times 10, tomorrow? How do we evaluate fund managers and entrepreneurs for their impact, and how do they decide which metrics are most important to the communities they serve, in addition to the investors that fund them?

This sort of active impact management has been a hallmark of our practice ever since we realized that there was an opportunity for the industry to do better. We have been thrilled to see that a number of fund managers, such as our colleagues at HCAP Partners, have been equally excited to take up the challenge of implementing active impact management practices alongside measurement practices—and we hope this is something aspiring investors and entrepreneurs will also consider in the future.

In thinking about meaningful metrics to guide management in the impact industry, we need to look closely at whether some of the metrics we have traditionally used to evaluate success accurately reflect or not what they purport to measure.

For instance, job creation is one of the primary activities the impact investment industry has pursued to address worldwide poverty, and hence "number of jobs created" is often cited as an antipoverty metric. In 2015, I had one of those embarrassing press moments in an otherwise fantastic article about Pi's work. A thoughtful, well-meaning journalist for *The Guardian* inadvertently quoted me out of context as saying: "Job creation is a meaningless metric." This was not the first time my candidness has gotten me into trouble. (Indeed, my sister, museum expert Nina Simon, and I were the first sibling pair to both win a prize at our high school graduation for "the outspoken defense of the rights of others"—my mother affectionately keeps the certificate framed on her desk and refers to it as the "big mouth award.") Job creation numbers do, of course, carry weight, but the metric of job creation is also a great example of why simple measurement, without greater thoughtfulness about management and actual systemic outcomes, limits our potential for impact.

The World Bank estimates that we will need 600 million jobs by 2020 to keep up with population growth globally—and 200 million of these jobs will be needed in developing economies.[3] Small and growing businesses (SGBs), the vehicle impact investors prefer second to microfinance in fostering job or livelihood creation, have been shown to be critically linked to increases in gross domestic product (GDP) and reductions in overall poverty in developing countries.[4] SGB growth is therefore supposed to help poor people through two mechanisms: it creates jobs, which provide much-needed income; and it encourages GDP growth, which, in theory, supports the overall economic health of a country and reduces poverty. But these suppositions have a few fatal flaws that need to be addressed before we can wholeheartedly support job creation as a strategy for global poverty reduction.

We live on a planet of finite resources. By design, GDP cannot grow infinitely. While in the short term it's nice to show impact investors graphs that trend up, you can't rely on short-term fixes for long-term global problems. This is particularly important for those of us thinking regionally and not just locally, given that, in the context of a global race to the bottom on wages and environmental standards, one country's success may mean another's ruin. For example, if a company moves to poor country X because the cost of doing business there is lower, it deprives poor country Y of the same jobs and drives down global wages overall. It's imperative that people who are focused on poverty reduction rethink GDP as a benchmark. It simply doesn't take into account all of the variables required for truly positive social and environmental impact.

In addition, although there may be a correlation between GDP increases and poverty reduction, evidence is inconclusive on GDP's correlation to inequality. Certainly, there are many examples of countries like India and Brazil, which, despite miraculous growth in GDP, remain ravaged by inequality and are home to the greatest number of poor people in the world. To take the extreme case, the United States has the highest GDP in the world—and in 2012, the top 1 percent of the US population received 93 percent of the income growth.

Very often, SGB development is an attempt to replicate the US model of a free-market economy internationally. Should we promote a model that enables such extreme inequalities to persist? As one International Monetary Fund economist commented in the *New York Times*, "when a handful of yachts become ocean liners while the rest remain lowly canoes, something is seriously amiss."[5] Indeed, focusing on job creation without an equal focus on equality just reinforces this dichotomy.

Most importantly, poverty is caused not just by a lack of jobs, but also by the proliferation of low-paying jobs. The International Labour Organization defines the active poor as those who are either working or looking for a job. In the case of developing countries, both the inactive and active poor suffer from similar rates of poverty. This suggests that, especially with the lack of social security, there is a driving compulsion for the poor to accept low-quality jobs that often do not lead to a substantial increase in income.

Among those in developing countries who are employed, 34.9 percent are living in moderate and extreme poverty. Almost a quarter of these workers are waged and salaried employees, while the rest are self-employed. Overall, this percentage reflects over 640 million waged and salaried workers who are living on less than $3.10 per day.[6]

Are these employed persons better off than their self-employed, equally poor counterparts? Or do they run a higher risk of income uncertainty, given that they are more likely to be economic migrants with limited access to productive means such as land? I will leave this question to the statisticians, but let's just assume, for the sake of argument, that living on under $3.10 a day is quite challenging whether you have been paid that $3.10 or generated it yourself. And I would assume that in both scenarios, your opportunities for advancement are minimal. Indeed, to borrow a phrase from the economist Gary Fields, we don't have a global unemployment problem; we have a global *employment* problem, in that the jobs we create are precisely what are keeping people poor.[7]

This is why organizations like the Aspen Network of Development Entrepreneurs have tried to define "quality" jobs, and others argue that we should not focus on jobs at all. Livelihoods can come from many places—employment is just one option. I once sat on a panel with indigenous leader Winona LaDuke, who shared with us that "lots of people come to the res[ervation] to talk about job development. We don't want FTEs [full-time equivalent jobs]. We don't want to leave the res to work for Walmart. We want the preservation of our historic ways of generating our livelihood." From her point of view, a narrow focus on jobs was a distraction from deeper issues of overall prosperity and autonomy.

Finally, the singular focus on job creation misses the critical differences between employment and assets. An individual's ability to amass wealth is based on a variety of factors beyond employment, such as inheritance, home ownership, and education. Although a job may provide a short-term income boost to a household, it would take generations to make up for the asset shortfall that family could be facing. Furthermore, assets are better indicators of inequality, reflecting limits to economic, social, and political mobility. For example, a black man in the United States makes, on average, 25 percent less than his white counterpart—but the more frightening statistic is that black families in the United States have *twenty times less assets* than white families.[8] Job creation might help address income distribution, but it does little to address asset distribution, and, by extension, long-term and often intergenerational poverty.

Let's take a step back from job creation to consider what it means to be poor. As I mentioned in Chapter 2, I define poverty as a lack of choice to live life in a way that respects your physical needs, cultural values, social and political context, and familial obligations. What constitutes poverty in this light of course varies country by country and region by region, which is why I invite impact investors to rethink the way in which we approach poverty reduction as if it were a simplistic economic equation. Consider the following questions:

> What if we focused not just on income, but on asset-building for individuals and communities?
> What if we focused on culturally appropriate livelihoods, rather than limiting our viewpoint to wage employment?
> What would it look like if we focused on equality just as much as we do growth?

If we thought through those questions, perhaps we would end up still considering job creation to be an important cornerstone of impact investment. Certainly, by broadening our thinking and our approach to address other essential criteria for sustainable growth in developing economies (or emerging domestic markets), we would feel a greater level of confidence that our impact investment dollars were really leading to global poverty reduction and more autonomous communities. And rather than simply measuring job creation, we could consider a much broader set of metrics, and, most importantly, engage in active management based on those metrics, in order to ensure that the outcomes in poverty reduction we sought were actually achieved.

How does managing toward the broader goal of poverty reduction, rather than just job creation, change how an enterprise looks? Two enterprises provide interesting examples.

Liberty & Justice is a holding company with a presence in the United States and across Africa with a strong focus on livelihoods and asset-building.[9] Cofounder Chid Liberty wanted to address the 90 percent unemployment rate in Liberia. So he built Africa's first fair trade factory—a clothing manufacturing facility employing over one hundred women. These women not only have access to high-quality jobs, but also own 49 percent of the factory, and are being trained to one day run it and fully own it themselves.

Investors in L&J participate in a US trading company that partners with factories in several countries across Africa and ensures that they comply with global quality standards. Chid's vision was not only to create good jobs for women, but to help close their asset gap. He has since expanded the Liberty & Justice brand to include Uniform, a line of clothing that also provides free school uniforms for Liberian children, and, most critically, kept women employed during the Ebola crisis.

Another company that has similarly worked to level the playing field for its workers is Namaste Solar, a Colorado-based solar company that is an employee-owned cooperative. Namaste's 160-plus employees are given the option to buy a share of the company, and there is an explicit salary scale specifying that the highest-paid employee cannot make more than six times the lowest-paid employee. This emphasis on democratic, cooperative ownership and a relatively equitable salary structure has produced a company of co-owners who really take responsibility for their company, which has significantly reduced turnover and helped drive profitability.

How does a *fund* look different when it manages toward poverty reduction and quality job creation, rather than just conventional wage job creation? This is even more complicated, since a fund has to tend to the welfare and address the practices of several companies simultaneously. But as Pi Investments found working alongside HCAP Partners, it is indeed possible.

Pi was interested in supporting HCAP Partners' deepening commitment to creating quality jobs within historically disadvantaged communities in the United States, going beyond job creation as traditionally conceived to consider factors such as a living wage, benefits, and ownership opportunities. The lessons Pi and HCAP learned will, I hope, provide some insight into how limited partners can work with general partners to encourage active impact management, not just measurement, and ensure that top impact funds can continue to innovate and set best practices within the field—no matter the sector or location.

IMPACT 1.0: QUALITY MEASUREMENT

HCAP Partners, previously known as Huntington Capital, was founded in 2000 with a mission to generate above-market returns while having a positive impact on underserved businesses and their communities. Its first two portfolios, Funds I and II, showed successful execution toward this objective, generating significant employment for underserved individuals, including women and people of color living in low- to moderate-income zip codes. HCAP has been consistently listed in the ImpactAssets 50, a selection of top fund managers in the field, and has been recognized for its effective impact measurement processes. Its 2013 impact report shared the following data:

» HCAP has invested $87 million across Funds I and II.

» Seventy-five percent of these portfolios meets Small Business Administration guidelines for traditionally underserved companies.

» Fifty percent of HCAP's portfolio companies are located in low- to moderate-income regions.

» These companies support 2,262 employees in a mix of new jobs and maintained jobs in otherwise disappearing sectors, such as manufacturing.

» Sixty-three percent of these employees are people of color.

» Forty-three percent of the employees are women.[10]

IMPACT 2.0: QUALITY MANAGEMENT

At Pi Investments, we knew that few funds in the United States focused on economic opportunity for historically disadvantaged communities, and thus we were intrigued to learn about HCAP Partners. It had an impressive track record and provided a relatively unique type of capital—mezzanine debt with upside potential—in an underserved segment of mid-sized companies.

At the same time, we were (and remain) hesitant to support investments in funds where the sole impact intention is job creation. Clearly, underserved communities with high unemployment rates need access to jobs. Unless we are enabling true innovation or demand generation, we can't do much more than move jobs from one zip code to another. And even when jobs are created in a low-income community, if they are low paying, then by definition they are *precisely* what keep these communities locked into cycles of poverty.

Rather than counting jobs, we were interested in the migration of low-quality jobs to high-quality jobs. From this perspective, we approached HCAP Partners to say that while we were very impressed with their impact measurement in carefully tracking job creation, we wanted to work with them to better address impact *outcomes*—ensuring that the jobs created actually led to a better quality of life. This project would entail working closely with portfolio companies not only on economic value creation—helping companies grow—but on "impact value creation"—helping companies grow in ways that also benefited their workers. The companies were collecting the required data, but they didn't necessarily know why. They were not receiving feedback on their practices or getting any coaching on how to improve them. And even if they wanted to treat their workers well, they didn't always have insight into what was most valuable to workers to enhance their quality of life, or know how to implement more aspirational standards.

The challenge of focusing on impact outcomes was not unique to HCAP Partners. Managers at funds like HCAP work tirelessly to achieve above-market-rate returns for their investors while satisfying a whole host of impact data requirements, such as Community Reinvestment Act criteria and IRIS indicators for their diverse investor base. But this approach to impact measurement is by nature highly focused on *outputs* rather than *outcomes and additionality*—the value that a particular fund manager is able to provide compared to others.

CREATING AN IMPACT MANAGEMENT SYSTEM

The founders of HCAP Partners believed in the strength of their metrics, but strategically they were interested in continuing to raise the bar. This meant being able to show how their investments were actually creating high-quality employment and ownership opportunities in order to reduce poverty in low- to moderate-income communities. They embraced the idea of an impact management framework and were open to collaborating with us on designing one. We were generalists with only inch-deep expertise in a variety of sectors, and we recognized that we had to educate ourselves on job quality if we were going to help HCAP Partners. Our first task was to make sure we were hearing the voices of low-income workers and prioritizing their needs.

We turned to Transform Finance, our natural partner, given my relationship as cofounder and our alignment of missions. Alongside supportive colleagues at the Ford Foundation, Transform Finance helped us interview leading workers' rights organizations and advocates—including Jobs with Justice, the Center for Labor Research and Education at the University of California at Berkeley, and The Partnership for Working Families—to identify top priorities for low-wage workers.[11]

While some priorities—such as health care and a living wage—were predictable, others surprised us. For example, low-wage workers surveyed nationally tended to value paid sick days even more than increases in compensation, and in particular, the ability to take time to support sick family members. As working professionals, we found it hard to fathom not being permitted to leave a job early to pick up a sick child from school, for example, but for most low-income workers in the United States, that is the reality. We also learned that worker-ownership, typically limited to tech companies, is a hugely motivating force and driver of productivity within companies across sectors. The insights provided by the organizations we consulted were a good reminder that as investors (people who are used to being the "experts"), we need to reach outside of our usual networks and ensure that our priority-setting reflects the perspective of beneficiaries.

Once we had a starting list of priorities (health care, paid sick days, a living wage, training and opportunities for advancement, and employee ownership or profit-sharing),[*] we asked Transform Finance to examine the economic impact of implementing such policies at companies. Given the commitment of HCAP Partners to delivering above-market performance—and the fact that a poorly performing company cannot create or maintain *any* jobs, high or low in quality—we knew this was of the utmost importance.

The good news is that the evidence overwhelmingly shows that treating workers well only enhances company performance—and, by extension, fund performance. Here's some of what we learned:

» *Paid sick-day provisions increase morale and productivity.* A 2014 study on Connecticut's paid sick days law—the first statewide policy in the nation—found that after the law was implemented in 2012, one-third of businesses reported improved worker morale, while 15 percent saw increased productivity and a reduction in the spread of

---

[*] In retrospect, we missed one—we should've also referenced the "Ban the Box" campaign, which asks employers to engage fair hiring practices when evaluating the applications of formerly incarcerated people. For instance, employers can choose not to run a background check until after a provisional offer letter has already been provided rather than asking on the initial application form, and consider more thoughtfully whether such history will actually impact the candidate's performance. This just goes back to the fact that social education is an ongoing activity—I know more now than I did when we began this work with HCAP! Engaging companies and funds around Ban the Box is now a regular part of our work.

illness. Moreover, only one in ten businesses reported a 3 percent or more increase in payroll cost, which gains in productivity and morale likely offset.[12]

» *Paid sick days prevent "presenteeism."* Presenteeism is the opposite of absenteeism: it refers to when sick workers report to work, but are unwell and unproductive. The business cost of workers showing up sick or incapacitated actually exceeds that of absenteeism by $160 billion annually, according to one study.[13]

» *Paying a living wage reduces turnover.* It's well established that turnover costs as much as 1.5 to 2.5 times an employee's annual salary.[14]

» *Paying a living wage reduces employee theft.* Employees paid higher wages are less likely to steal and, perhaps even more interestingly, less likely to collude with others to steal.[15]

» *Worker ownership decreases turnover, increases productivity, and increases overall commitment to the well-being of the enterprise.* Anyone who has ever held stock options knows this intuitively. According to research from Rutgers University, implementing employee ownership leads to a 4 percent permanent increase in productivity and a 2 percent increase in shareholder value.[16]

Convinced that we could offer approaches that would enhance both the fund's social impact and its financial return, we worked with HCAP Partners to create a "Gainful Jobs Approach" to impact management using a "floor and ladder" framework. This approach requires all companies in the fund to meet basic minimum requirements (which we defined together) in five areas—living wage, health care, paid leave, opportunities for advancement, and employee ownership—

or show an action plan for achieving this minimum "floor" within a year of the investment. The companies would then set annual targets to climb the "ladder of goals," with support as needed from the HCAP Partners management team and consultants.

Just as any fund checks in with management at least quarterly to assess financial performance and try to help support key goals, such a framework makes it clear to the company how it can improve its impact performance and guides the fund in its work with the underlying portfolio. It also assures limited partners in funds (commonly referred to as "LPs") that, rather than just measuring outputs after the fact, the fund is actually actively creating "impact value" alongside financial value.

IMPACT IMPLEMENTATION

The HCAP team felt the framework would enable them to put their values more concretely into action. They understood that such an explicit impact emphasis would give them a competitive advantage compared to other funds, attracting founders who truly believed in treating their workers fairly and wanted a values-aligned investor. Impact-oriented LPs like the Heron Foundation, Blue Haven Initiative, and the Northwest Area Foundation had already been supporting HCAP Partners' work, and this framework would just take things to the next level.

At this point we were still being courted, and hence we had some slight hesitations about the possibility that the managers were simply telling us what we wanted to hear in their efforts to bring in new impact investor partners; or that, even if their commitment was genuine, the companies in their portfolio could still ignore their requests. We also knew that the investment commitment we could facilitate would be relatively small compared to that of other institutions investing in the fund, and that the management team would rightly not commit to implementing changes that didn't serve HCAP Partners' mission of providing above-market returns alongside strong impact. Our trust in the team's competency and professionalism was a major factor.

What ultimately convinced us that HCAP Partners was truly committed to excellence in both financial return and social impact was that its management team raised very legitimate concerns about how the companies it funded would implement the framework, and brought forward some innovative ideas for trying to ensure that implementation would be effective. The team proved equally concerned about execution, and wanted to make sure their commitment was both realistic and in accordance with their values.

Since HCAP Partners is primarily a debt provider and thus has limited ownership of companies, the fund is, by nature, a minority investor with limited control and/or influence over its portfolio companies. HCAP Partners didn't want a company to take its money and accept job-quality provisions it didn't really plan to implement. While impact practices are often written into loan agreements, unless a fund manager wants to actually trigger a default provision based on a company's inability to produce impact outcomes (an unlikely scenario), such provisions are extremely difficult to enforce.

HCAP Partners also works with mid-market companies across sectors that are not classically defined "social enterprises," and hence impact is not necessarily written into their

DNA. As a fund it therefore could potentially have much greater impact than others by moving these companies along the impact spectrum, an exciting prospect but also an additional challenge in introducing new ideas around job quality.

HCAP's proposed solution was to incentivize company management to implement impact practices, focusing on providing carrots rather than covenant-related requirements. Given the fact that its debt is structured with various kicker functions to provide upside (meaning that HCAP Partners can make more money if the company is successful), one way that HCAP Partners thought to reasonably encourage companies to implement changes was to provide additional financial incentives. What form that incentive would ultimately take is still to be determined, but it is this sort of innovative thinking about impact management that will lead the sector to strong outcomes, beyond mere outputs.

HCAP Partners also wanted to ensure that it developed sufficient expertise about implementing job-quality practices so that it could be a credible advisor to its portfolio companies. It committed to hiring a full-time impact associate, who is now leading its work on impact management strategy and supporting portfolio companies on an ongoing basis.

Both in expressing their justifiable reservations about the workability of our proposed framework and in coming up with innovative ways to address them, the managers at HCAP Partners proved that they were committed to enhancing HCAP's impact management practices with or without us—and perhaps even more extensively than we could have imagined. Our missions were clearly aligned.

We are now proud supporters of a fund that we believe has the potential to lead the way in impact management practices, and, most importantly, ensure that thousands of working people in the United States—notably women and people of color—can move from a place of poverty to stability.

For instance, one of HCAP's investments since the implementation of the job-quality initiative has been Noribachi, an LED light manufacturer in Los Angeles. Noribachi's founders have been very focused on job quality, both as a means of cultivating a quality workforce and as a reflection of their social values. They believe in providing people with careers, not just jobs, and have implemented some related practices that are unusual in manufacturing:

» All team members are employees with benefits; there are no contractors.
» All team members have stock options and receive financial education on their value—not just managers.
» Team members can test out different factory-floor and office jobs without any salary penalty as a way of assessing their core competencies and interests.
» Company finances are open book, and all managers have an open door policy.
» Education is ongoing and open to all—including a weekly 6:00 a.m. math class led by the CEO (a PhD mathematician).

Despite having a choice of capital providers, Noribachi's founders were particularly excited to work with HCAP Partners because they shared HCAP's vision on job quality—this in itself was confirmation that HCAP's commitment had become a competitive advantage for the fund itself in pursuing deals.

HCAP's journey, thoughtfulness about impact, and willingness to lean on LPs and nonprofit partners for support can and should be a model for funds in the sector. Still, at the end of the day, there is only so much that one fund, or one LP, can do to support the improvement of a whole industry. Both at Pi and within HCAP, we were thrilled that Transform Finance subsequently took this initial work and expanded it into an initiative to drive more impact investments domestically into quality job creation across the industry.

For fund managers and aspiring practitioners, the burden is on us to gauge the difference between outputs and outcomes as we assess the impact potential of potential investees. Instead of focusing on measurement systems alone, we can help shape impact management systems. Investees, just like investors, are in this business because they want to drive positive change, not just measure impact in the rearview mirror. So I leave you with this question: Will you drive your impact looking backward, or forward?

ten

REAL IMPACT AT SCALE

WE'VE NOW WALKED THROUGH A NEW APPROACH TO impact investment and outlined a management structure to implement it. The next natural question about the Transform Finance principles and approach is this: Can we actually implement this at scale, or are we just fetishizing a few high-impact projects? Indeed, being thoughtful about our personal practices as bridge-builders is part of this on a micro level. On a macro level, we can try to be more thoughtful about the questions we emphasize as we scale as an industry. And then there's the step in the middle: Even as we all work together to scale a smarter, more impactful industry, what can we do now at the portfolio level to start making more transformative investments?

As all investors know, it's quite a challenge to build a portfolio that follows a cohesive investment thesis, especially across asset classes. Several reports have shown that you can indeed have impact across a portfolio while achieving or beating market rates of return, though generally with a very broad impact focus.[1] Would it be possible to build a 100 percent impact portfolio, as pioneers in the field have already done, but with more of a social justice emphasis, as embodied in the Transform Finance principles?

This is the question we sought to answer in 2012 when we began to support an extremely thoughtful member of the Pritzker family committed to social justice. She and her husband are the type of people you may be secretly jealous of for their ability to live so graciously. They always take a mug to the coffee shop, bike just about everywhere (with kids in tow), are engaged with social justice issues, and in general are extremely intentional about their everyday life decisions, in a quiet way that is simply thoughtful, not obnoxious.

And yet, their investment portfolio didn't match them at all. They were, financially, like vegans wearing bright pink mink coats. It wasn't their fault; they were simply invested in the same financial products that anyone who walks into a typical financial institution will be sold. Their cash was kept at a big-name bank notorious for funding mining and land grabs in South Africa, as well as for its leading role in the mortgage crisis that left thousands of US homeowners on the streets. Like most investors, they also had significant holdings in the stock market, where among hundreds of publicly held companies there are crowd-pleasers like fracking operations, private prisons, tobacco companies, and more banks doing more deplorable things. You may or may not have this family's level of wealth, but your investment portfolio likely looks a lot like theirs did.

They approached their traditional financial advisor to see what they could do to shift their portfolio and found themselves underwhelmed by the product offerings on the market, which had very general approaches to impact. They realized that if they wanted to fundamentally change their investing approach, they were going to need a comprehensive strategy—and that they would also need help to get there outside of the traditional financial advisor landscape.

They first did what many do when trying something new—they approached someone who they knew and trusted. Aner Ben-Ami was an old friend of the family who shared their worldview about social responsibility; given their social leanings, he was also one of few people they knew who had an MBA. After business school, Aner had gone on to a job at Boston Consulting Group (BCG). As a consultant, you have to very quickly become as expert as you can on a topic you may have started out knowing very little about, and then help organize information in a way that helps others make decisions—a skill set very applicable to investing. In September 2012, Aner left BCG and agreed to come on board to help the family's financial advisor figure out an action plan. This initial work led to the founding of Pi Investments.

As part of his initial effort to learn about the social investment field, Aner joined Toniic. I was Toniic's CEO at the time, and as part of their introduction to impact investment, he and the family began reading what I had written over the years about the subject. These writings expressed the Transform Finance philosophy and advocated for the type of systemic change they were looking to support. We quickly saw how values-aligned our outlooks were. When I announced in January 2013 that I was transitioning from Toniic in order to pursue my value set more specifically, Pi was one of the first places I shyly went to express my interest in joining the team. I was thrilled to make that change official by the summer and begin my work with Aner and the family.

We then got to work defining a strategy. We needed to, alongside the family and their advisors, define our impact focus, set return targets, and ultimately, assist in building a portfolio. In 2016, the family largely completed the transition from a 0 percent impact to a close to 100 percent impact portfolio, with over forty-five private investments supported. With the family's support, we are happy to share with aspiring impact investors some of what we've learned in the process.

The first thing any impact investor needs to do is define the focus: What kind of impact do you want to have? For some this is a very simple and intuitive choice. An investor may be particularly passionate about the environment, or women's rights, or education, or a particular place. But for many who view the world from a social justice lens, it's hard to pick a single issue among so many that are worthy, especially when the issues are fundamentally interconnected.

You can build a fantastic school in a poor community, for example, but if children don't have access to a proper breakfast, or health care, they will not be prepared to take advantage of that great education. If systemic racism or sexism or homophobia is still endemic to the community—or to the institution itself—the children may not, depending on their appearance or gender or sexual preference, receive a culturally appropriate education, or may even, through implicit bias, be provided less support than others within the same institution.

And if greenhouse gas emissions continue to grow, that school might be underwater within a decade.

This sort of thinking can incite one of two reactions. The first is to throw up our hands, rightfully proclaim that social change is damn complicated, and stick to things we know and that we see are having positive, short-term impacts. In the investment world, they say, "No one gets fired for buying General Electric." Perhaps the social justice equivalent is "No one feels bad for donating to the food bank." The other response is to say: "Let's look at the systemic *reasons* why people globally keep losing on so many fronts. Why is it that on a planet with so many resources and natural intelligence, we can move an orange from Florida to Japan in a day, but haven't prioritized, or figured out, how to keep people from suffering?"

Aner and I spent significant initial energy to clearly articulate a worldview that would lead us toward a more systemic way of addressing impact for Pi, and we have to update this worldview consistently as new influences expand, or complicate, our understanding. We came up with a standard one-pager that we send to potential partners to explain our objectives (reproduced in the box).

OBJECTIVES AT PI INVESTMENTS

We seek to address several structural challenges that reinforce an extractive economy:

- *Shareholder primacy misaligns incentives.* The notion that a corporation's sole purpose is to maximize returns for its shareholders treats working people and the planet as costs that have to be minimized, rather than recognized as assets and key long-term stakeholders.

—continues—

—continued—

- *Remote and limited ownership leads to wealth extraction.* Business relationships are anonymous and lead to a limited, short-term emphasis on financial returns that are unsustainable in the long run. Ownership—and by extension, financial prosperity—is limited to those who have access to resources. Financial return is typically based on wealth extraction from historically disadvantaged communities or from the planet's nonrenewable resources.
- *Infinite growth models are incompatible with a finite planet.* An overemphasis on short-term financial return leads to a pursuit of perpetual growth that is incompatible with finite global resources. This leads to an overemphasis on engineering our way out of our current environmental crisis, and in the private markets, companies and assets have to be sold to maximize returns for investors, with little regard for mission preservation.
- *Limited leadership stunts our creativity to address global challenges.* Impact investment is being defined by investors, fund managers, and other intermediaries and entrepreneurs, with very limited engagement or direct accountability to those being served.

We support investments in vehicles that promote a generative, inclusive economy by:

- Making sure to add more value than is extracted from both people and the planet
- Focusing on fulfilling human needs rather than creating new ones through ethical production, reducing overall resource consumption
- Incorporating communities in design, governance and ownership of enterprises, and enabling their collective activity through advocacy and engagement
- Creating direct, transparent investment opportunities that supports ownership that is both broad and deep within a local context

-continued-

- Balancing risk and return to investors, entrepreneurs and communities
- Exploring investment structures that encourage companies to maintain and deepen their mission focus as they grow

The approach to investment we outline gives us the advantage of being able to look for transformative projects in any sector or geography, helping build up a portfolio across sectors that, collectively, is designed to encourage structural shifts in economies, and to do away with inequality and economic incentives to consume or otherwise destroy the natural environment. Regardless of the sector or geography, we are consistently and respectfully looking for ways to expand the impact of a project, and, in particular, for ways to engage in intentional intersectionality between sectors. For instance, it's great if a project addresses food waste, but why not seize the opportunity to address food access for low-income people at the same time?

Because impact investment is a relatively new, growing field, the number of values-aligned investment opportunities connected to any particular mission is still limited. Having a focus that's too narrow can make it challenging to implement a 100 percent portfolio approach: you can only invest so much, for instance, in food justice in Cleveland across asset classes—so our broad but deep focus enables us to help fill out a portfolio.

Our approach also attracts exceptional entrepreneurs and fund managers who want help pushing the envelope on impact; they seek us out as "value-add" partners because of our particular expertise. Entrepreneurs often know intuitively exactly the impact they seek, but they rely on us to better articulate this message to others and deepen the mechanism by which they execute on that impact.

There are, of course, disadvantages to our approach as well. In exploring such a broad spectrum of sectors and geographical areas, we recognize that while we can educate ourselves quickly, we will never be the experts on any particular sector. This likely makes us less effective in our diligence, and we have less access to some of the best deals, as we likely do not represent the highest value-add investor within a sector. We also need to steer clear of investments that rely on technologies that we anticipate not fully grasping, or that we aren't able to effectively compare with alternatives, such as biodigesters or new desalinization techniques.

Another disadvantage is that investing with others becomes more complicated. We often confuse our peers, who are used to recommending deals to others based on what they've done before. Once we've facilitated one food deal, for example, all of a sudden we get sent twenty food deals, even if our purpose for supporting the initial food deal was less about the sector than it was about the transformative approach. We also wind up having to be a part of a large number of investor communities to stay current on a variety of sectors, which involves a lot more time, travel, and relationship management than staying current on just one or two sectors.

However, despite these disadvantages, as more investors start to engage with the Transform Finance framework it gets easier for us to find peers who are equally excited about systemic change, whether they aim to achieve it by diving deep into a sector or by seeking investments as broadly as we do. In 2014, Transform Finance launched the Transform Finance Investor Network at the White House as a nonprofit educational initiative, with members seeking to dedicate $556 million toward transformative impact. That amount has now increased to over $2 billion, reflecting the growing engagement of multiple investors, from individuals to institutions, that are interested in enhancing their impact.[2]

Once an impact framework has been prepared, the second question an impact investor must ask is, "How much money do I want to make?"

People often skip this step. The first instinct for most investors is, "Well, of course—let's make as much money as possible, as fast as possible!" But the impact investor is compelled to ask a new set of questions: How much money do I ultimately *need* to make? Is it the quantity that I have—meaning, is it okay if we break even? Is it more? Or is it perhaps less—meaning, is it okay to spend down the investment pool as a form of philanthropy? If I had more money, what would I do with it? Does how I acquired the money make a difference to my thinking? Do I have any legal restrictions in what I'm allowed to do? In what time frame do I need the money? If a typical fund earns returns in ten years, do I care if it takes twelve to get my money back? Would I occasionally take less financial return if I was really excited about what a project was doing in the world?

For foundations, this may be a pretty simple question, as foundations legally need to give away 5 percent of their assets each year.[3] They also need to spend a reasonable amount to hire staff and support their work, and they need to keep up with inflation. Taking all of those factors into consideration, they will likely seek an 8 percent return that is relatively stable, rather than looking for riskier but higher returns. This framework is often called the "endowment model" of investing. Foundations may adopt one of two mindsets—they may want to "spend down" and diminish their resources, taking the view that sitting on their assets when climate change and inequality might end the world in fifty years is not a viable strategy; or they may decide to play a longer-term game, in which case they will want to grow their asset base even beyond their current resources in order to give more grants in the future.

For individuals, making this decision is a much more challenging, personal, and complex endeavor. An investor who comes from a situation where financial resources have been limited may want to accumulate capital in order to have more freedom of choice in life, both presently and for future generations. Another investor coming from a background of wealth may want to preserve that wealth for future generations, or may want to disseminate it back into society.

For working-class individuals who rightfully fear the decline of the social safety net in their old age, maximizing investment returns to ensure some kind of retirement is an essential objective. For many people, particularly people of color and people in the Global South who have been systemically locked out of wealth accumulation structures for centuries, any opportunity to engage in investment and entrepreneurship can provide a way to level the playing field.

For people who have inherited money, the origin of the money may factor greatly into how they want to treat it, and even legally how they can treat it. There are a number of next-generation wealth holders who recognize the ways in which the resources bestowed upon them may have hurt numerous others along the way—because of fossil fuel development, slavery, worker exploitation or low-quality job provision, and the like. They may view it as their obligation to use those resources to try and correct some of these historical wrongs, and voluntarily attempt to do so through collaborative grant-making or investment practices. Resource Generation, a nonprofit organization that brings together progressive young people with wealth to explore these issues together, is particularly good for those who are wrestling with how to understand their own wealth and how to leverage it for social good.

Some trust structures legally require beneficiaries to preserve the money; they cannot give it all away even if they want to do so. In these cases the beneficiaries can still choose whether they want to maximize wealth, or maximize impact within the constraint of passing the regulator's test of reasonably attempting to preserve the capital.

Like most elements of transformative finance, the point here is not that one answer will solve all our challenges—but that it's important to ask the question, to realize that it has more than one answer, and to answer it in a way that feels fair and accountable to you.

The traditional impact investor will prioritize maximizing financial return, and then, as a secondary priority, set constraints on *how* that return may be maximized—in terms of what kinds of projects, sectors, or level of risk reflect his or her values, expertise, and comfort zone. No one wants to make a bad investment; nor does it help communities when projects fail. Traditional investors typically exclude from consideration, however, projects that might make a perfectly fine return, or even a more dependable one than they could count on in traditional markets, but at a slightly lower rate than what is considered "market." Market rate is an incredibly slippery concept, however, and it's often based on the financial sector's delusions of grandeur rather than on actual data, as noted in Chapter 2.

For Pi, we use traditional market indexing techniques to evaluate the portfolio's financial performance, and we acknowledge that markets tend to go up over time despite the boom-and-bust cycles capitalism is designed to facilitate, in part due to the value of creative destruction. Our instinct, however, is that steady, thoughtful growth makes for a healthier economy that is better for everyone in the long run. So while we currently support a traditional asset allocation for Pi Investments, we do anticipate over time diving even more deeply into the question of asset allocation and reasonable benchmarks. And, accordingly, we are more likely to look for deals and funds that project reasonable growth paths, rather than to suggest wild bets on companies that will either grow big or go bust.

Our mandate at Pi was to define a strategy to preserve the historical capital and add a small amount of additional financial return, rather than to maximize financial return, which led to a framework similar to the "endowment model" explained above. This mandate certainly requires us to have financial discipline in our investment identification, but it also gives us the latitude to intentionally pursue investments based on their impact, rather than their short-term profitability, as long as they fulfill some minimum standards to ensure the portfolio overall achieves its financial objectives.

Now that we had an impact framework, and an overall return objective for the portfolio, our next step was to break this up into impact and financial objectives for each asset class and set an overall asset allocation: meaning the framework by which investors choose how much money to put into different types of investments, from cash to bonds to stocks to venture capital and other private investments. We took the following steps to figure out a strategy.

Financial Strategy: First, we worked with a third-party advisor to design the overall asset allocation. This step generally involves a fairly standard, tech-heavy process of analyzing thousands of future scenarios and trying to come up with the optimal structure for achieving our objectives. Like all future modeling—as they say, "garbage in, garbage out"—it must be managed very carefully. While inherently imperfect, such scenarios are the best tool the financial industry has, and they do provide a useful starting place. So with this analysis in hand, we had an initial sense of the return targets per asset class for the portfolio most likely to yield the overall target return.

Given our impact priorities, we tweaked the standard asset allocation design in two ways: by excluding hedge funds and MLPs (master limited partnerships), despite their traditionally high financial performance. Our feeling was that these financial tools were structurally up to no good: hedge funds, because of their lack of transparency; and MLPs, because of their support of the fossil fuel industry. The advisor felt that we could still achieve our overall return targets without these two instruments, and helped adjust the allocation accordingly.

As always, where the rubber hits the road is where things start to get interesting. Armed with a return target for an asset class, how do we start evaluating potential opportunities? We realized that we needed to go a step further than the traditional asset allocation framework in our methodology.

Hypothetically, let's say the return target for investments in private equity is 10 percent. Three opportunities come across our desk in a given month—one with projected returns at 8 percent, one at 11 percent, and one at 13 percent.

How do we decide which one to pursue? We realized that human instinct is always to say, "Go for the 13 percent!" But given the fact that each opportunity had a different risk profile and a different impact profile, the shiniest object from a return perspective was not necessarily the best fit for our actual mandate.

We thought about the fact that we could actually support all three investments and still remain on target. We just needed to be thoughtful in budgeting for each type, and know exactly why and when we were choosing to recommend a lower-return product. Some would call this "giving up" return—instead, we wanted to focus on having the return be contextually appropriate and achievable for each investment. So we took the private allocation (including equity, debt, and real assets) and divided it into the following three subcategories:

1. *High projected return, low financial risk, medium impact.* This category includes well-established funds that offer something more positive impact-wise than a traditional financial product, but are not yet particularly transformative. Typically these were also funds we hoped to engage with to enhance their impact.

2. *High projected return, more financial risk, high impact.* This category often includes funds directed by first-time fund managers, or opportunities reflecting strategies that, for whatever reason, implicitly feel more risky, but are very aligned with our mandate in terms of their intended level of impact. In general, given the fact that many impact investment funds are first-time

or smaller funds, we felt it was essential to have an allocation to this bucket established in the portfolio.

3. *Low projected return, lower financial risk, high impact.* This category generally includes funds that have a great track record of consistent, below-market, but reasonable returns and a unique impact story. We recognize that, particularly investing under the endowment model, these type of investments can be very useful because they achieve targeted impact while minimizing volatility.

Noticeably absent from this list is "medium return, medium impact"—the impact investor's version of "meh." Our feeling was that these funds were not helpful in advancing the impact investment conversation. Their returns weren't consistent enough to encourage people to jump into the field, and their impact wasn't compelling enough (in our assessment) to represent a model we wanted to help scale. Hence we have evolved what we sometimes call a "barbell" strategy, one heavy on both ends of the scale, supporting either very financially successful funds and companies with longer track records, where we feel we can help expand their impact, or funds and companies that are riskier or pursue a lower return strategy but achieve really exceptional impact.

This strategy has led to some tough conversations over time with fund managers and entrepreneurs. These actors are fairly well accustomed to accepting that an investor disagrees with their financial strategy. But hearing that an investor disagrees with their social impact strategy may provoke a much more challenging conversation, as the nature of that strategy is often deeply personal, reflecting each party's individual values and life commitment to impact. When we say no to an investment opportunity, we try as part of our overall commitment to transparency and accountability to be very specific about our reasons, including explaining what we do or do not see as effective in their impact strategy. We know some people may take offense at our opinion, but we feel that open dialogue is essential in growing our field. We would encourage more investors to have these sorts of tough conversations with their current and potential investees.

Impact Strategy: Once we developed an asset-class approach, the next step was to establish clearly what "high impact" actually meant to us, and thus when we wanted to be more flexible on the return profile of a project.

Though our approach was sector neutral, that didn't mean that any old opportunity for impact in agriculture, microfinance, clean energy, health, small business development, or housing would qualify as being right for our approach. As my partner Aner always says, for us it's not about the "what," but about the "how." Did an agricultural project empower small farmers, or did it steal land out from under them? Did a microfinance project provide real opportunities for income development, or just put people into unsustainable debt? In evaluating impact investment opportunities, we apply our impact lens not just to the specific project but to the sector itself, first asking this question: What are the sorts of interventions within this particular sector that will lead to systemic change?

This approach helps address the question of impact measurement for very diverse portfolios by distilling a key set of criteria that can help us evaluate the long-term, systemic impact of an intervention regardless of the sector. We can then supplement this more universal assessment with specific criteria related to that sector and that particular type of intervention. Here are four fundamental questions we ask to help us evaluate any private investment through our impact lens:

1. *Communities:* How are local communities engaged in the project or process represented by this investment? Are their needs identified and incorporated into design, governance, and/or ownership? By how much are communities better off as a result? Are critical communities or sectors being reached?
2. *Best Practices:* Is the fund managing its assets according to best practices, as defined by local communities, NGOs, and advocacy groups in the local context—not just by the industry itself?
3. *Value-Add:* What is the social/environmental value added by the particular manager? How does this compare to the base case of the asset being held by conventional managers or by competitor "impact" managers? Are they following best-in-class practices? Do they offer particular expertise about social and environmental practices, or hold relationships important to their investees? How are they going beyond impact measurement to active management?
4. *Transition Plan:* What is the expected transition plan or exit strategy for the assets, and how will their social/environmental value be maintained?

Before assessing potential investees' answers to these questions, and to other questions specific to particular sectors, one has to make some judgment calls about what actually makes for good impact. This goes back to what I consider to be key in my "qualification" as an impact investor: just as I will canvass a field and work to maintain a network to identify the best investment opportunities, I need to be equally skilled in having the networks and information available to make smart decisions about impact—especially when I know that someone down the line is going to be directly affected by the decision I make.

We start out by talking to the experts in that particular field, with "expert" broadly defined. We generally aim to talk to at least two experts in each of these three categories when evaluating any sector:

Members of the Impacted Community or Users of the Particular Service

This category might include women who have taken out microfinance loans, farmers who live in communities suffering from land grabs in the name of renewable energy development, or families struggling to choose between public and private education offerings.

Investors often skip this step, and try to understand the experience of people with very different life circumstances by checking in with the entrepreneur and conducting desk research as their primary tools. While I'm sure many investors have a great capacity for empathy, there is nothing that can beat lived experience in understanding the impact of a particular intervention. While one person's experience certainly can't be extrapolated to an intervention that might be intended to impact a million people, it can help you understand that intervention's interplay with other factors that make up a person's overall quality of life.

Ideally, these conversations take place after relationships of trust have already been established, not during a one-off diligence trip, where there may be all sorts of dynamics that make it hard for a community member to tell his or her full story. To reiterate a primary point of this book: this step does not work well if you do not make an effort to connect with social movements and support them on their terms an ongoing priority. It's challenging to gain access to information critical to evaluating impact unless rapport has been established before seeking specific input. This kind of direct engagement also helps an investor or entrepreneur understand the broader context of why this intervention is even necessary—and hence if the intervention is a Band-Aid solution or a structural one.

Exceptional Entrepreneurs or Fund Managers

These people tend to have a broad range of experience across interventions and thus can best evaluate the financial and impact potential of various solutions. They also tend to have the most accurate information about just how difficult it is (or isn't) to implement a particular solution, and may have already tried and abandoned several models on their way to effective intervention. Their experience can safeguard you from investing in projects that replicate mistakes someone else has already made.

Investor Partners Who Focus on a Particular Area

Like entrepreneurs, but with an even wider and longer view, investors have typically thoroughly canvassed a field before deciding to place their first investments. They also may have done considerable work evaluating the technological risks of certain interventions in a way that a sector-neutral investor will not have had the capacity to explore.

How do you organize such a multifaceted canvas in practice? I can provide examples from our disparate experiences in two sectors: renewable energy development and microfinance. I'll note that although sometimes, if we need to do a concerted sector effort on a tight timeline (like we did for sustainable forestry), we might conduct such a canvass over the course of a month. In other cases, as in these two particular examples, we built our understanding in a series of slow-burning conversations over several years; each then involved some more intense activity as we evaluated live investment opportunities.

In the case of renewable energy, in general our objective was to rank solutions and opportunities across multiple types of interventions. Hence we made sure that we connected with people who were experienced across household systems, microgrids, and utility-scale energy development. Table 2 gives a sense of who we connected with and the perspectives each provided.

For microfinance, we specifically tried not only to tap people from communities in which the particular investments we were evaluating were proposed, but, given the contentiousness of the sector, also to make sure we talked to the strongest advocates and naysayers possible (see Table 3).

One might reasonably ask why any of these parties would want to share their hard-earned knowledge for free with a generalist who is essentially free-riding on their hard work. This is often a frustrating issue for entrepreneurs, who are often expected to freely give their time to investors, even if an investment is nowhere in sight.

TABLE 2. Due-Diligence Perspectives: Renewable Energy

Perspectives:	Topics:		
	Lanterns and Home Systems	*Microgrids*	*Utility Scale*
Community	Mexico: living in town with no electricity	Kenya and Rwanda: site visits with microgrid company	Brazil: living in favela with frequent power outages
Entrepreneur	Site visit with M-Kopa in Kenya	Site visit with PowerGen in Kenya	Site visit with Gigawatt Global in Rwanda
Investor	Blue Haven: home system investor	Prelude: microgrid investor	GVAC: experience across utility and microgrid

TABLE 3. Due-Diligence Sources: Microfinance

Perspective	Advocate	Naysayer
Community/beneficiary	Clients of Women's Initiative for Self-Employment in the United States, and D-Miro in Ecuador	World Social Forum participants
Fund manager / Practitioners	Matt Flannery, cofounder of Kiva; Luca Torre, cofounder of GAWA; Jonathan Lewis, founder of Micro-Credit Enterprises	Hugh Sinclair, author of *Confessions of a Microfinance Heretic*
Investors	The world's largest individual investor in microfinance	Anonymous investor with a decade of experience

It's important even as a generalist to find ways to provide value for others when seeking information, even if in that moment it may be challenging to identify the specific value-add you can offer. Andy Lower, formerly president of the Eleos Foundation, used to set the standard of making sure he spent as much time providing useful feedback as he did in taking an entrepreneur's time, whether while evaluating a potential investment or in seeking general feedback on a particular theme. In our work, we can point to two areas of practice—our experience in developing alternative terms to better match impact companies who are not heading toward an IPO or acquisition, and our experience in helping companies identify models for community engagement in design, governance, and ownership—where we may be able to assist the entrepreneur whose expertise we are equally seeking. We have also found that entrepreneurs often appreciate the depth of our on-the-ground experience. For instance, in a recent, relatively large transaction with a company working in Africa, we discovered that despite representing the smallest investor in the syndicate, we were the only ones who had actually set foot on the continent! We had thought visiting Africa was a fairly basic prerequisite for investing there, but our experience turned out to be a unique value-add.

Analyzing and codifying the information you get and the opinions you hear as you canvass experts can be an intense project. How do you take diverse opinions and turn them into something useful? Aner and I devised an overly simplistic impact rating system that exemplifies the terrible subjectivity implicit in making decisions about impact. We should note that we also have a much more robust impact measurement and management system that we've developed in-house to address specific opportunities. This simple system is nevertheless our starting point for diligence. It has three categories:

GOOD: Is the intervention at least somewhat better than status quo, with limited potential to cause harm, even if not fully transformative?

BETTER: Does the intervention create some sort of systemic change—in other words, does it get to the heart of the problem?

BEST: Does the intervention not only create systemic change around that issue, but also ensure that recipient communities receive their fair share of the financial value of the transaction? Are they engaged in terms of design, governance, and ownership?

In the case of renewable energy in the Global South, for instance, here's what we gleaned from the experts and how we lined it up to guide our work:

GOOD: Home systems that charge people less than the cost of kerosene while providing significantly more energy and services. Largely used for consumptive activity, like TVs, rather than productive activity, like water pumps, these systems are nice to have and far safer and cleaner than kerosene, but do not solve the long-term energy access issue. (In all fairness, some systems can be expanded over time to provide greater energy capacity, but they do require additional investment.) They also have the potential to be extractive in that it's very easy to offer the user a price that is cheaper than the terrible incumbent, without actually pushing to provide the service in a way that fairly balances the interests of investors, entrepreneurs, and communities.

BETTER: Microgrid systems, grid extension systems, or grid-sized projects that replace dirty energy sources. Given that 70 percent of those living without access to energy are actually not "off-grid" but simply "under grid"—i.e., they live within a kilometer of a grid, but just lack access to it—sometimes the best intervention is just to get more lines on the system and clean up its energy source. In other areas, like hilly Rwanda, installing a microgrid may actually be a cheaper long-term solution. In both cases, private companies need to be thoughtful about how to partner with governments and keep energy access public, open to all at affordable rates, and not just the wealthiest community members.

BEST: Companies in the "better" category that are being especially thoughtful about community engagement in design, governance, and ownership. Examples include a microgrid company like Virunga in Kenya that seeks to transition assets to community ownership after investors have received their return, or a utility-scale company like Gigawatt Global, working across Africa and in Palestine, that pushes more value down to beneficiary communities by offering high rents to community institutions, such as schools, that provide the land or otherwise serve as host sites for their solar installations. [Grupo Yansa, discussed in Chapter 6, is another great example of a company in the "best" category.]

In the case of some sectors that are rife with "impact washing," where we are unable to identify many positive companies or initiatives, this scale gets modified to "good, bad, and ugly." We tend to avoid interventions in such sectors at all, unless we feel extremely certain that an innovative entrepreneur or company has devised an intervention likely to make a really positive impact.

This was where we landed when it came to the microfinance sector, and why we specifically limited our investment activity in that area. We did choose to support some players that we felt landed in the "good" category and seemed to have the potential to push the sector in a better direction overall. In adopting this position, we may be accused of letting the perfect be the enemy of the good, but we feel that our intention is to highlight the good, and then encourage it to be the "best" it can be.

Investors often talk about "downside protection," which refers to what an entrepreneur or fund manager is doing to protect from negative financial outcomes. Similarly, as impact investors we think a lot about "impact downside protection," by which we mean how fund managers and entrepreneurs attempt to ensure that what they think is a good intervention won't end up ultimately hurting people.

Ironically, we have often found that the greatest impact downside risk exists in sectors intended to help people, such as financial services. Hence, we will sometimes choose not to support funds that are clearly labeled "impact" unless we trust their diligence when it comes to impact downside protection. Indeed, funds that are considered to be in the impact category simply based on the sectors they engage in, rather than on a deeper analysis, can be the riskiest. On the other hand, we have supported some investments in funds that specifically intend to make some portion of their investments in enterprises or technologies that are perhaps pleasant for the world, but do not seek to solve a major social or environmental problem. We figure that the impact downside potential of a file-sharing service or music program, for example, is far more neutral than that of a misguided attempt to help the poor—and while in general we seek the most positive interventions possible, we prefer neutral to negative!

The final question is what to do with the information we glean from canvassing a particular sector. There are two predominant outcomes.

First, the results enable us to pose more informed, more specific questions to entrepreneurs and fund managers in the sector. For instance, because we've learned that there is greater land-grab potential for utility-scale wind projects than for microgrid solar, we focus our impact questions differently in different types of interventions.

Second, the results help guide our approach to the use of risk capital. For instance, we might recommend debt, or other forms of lower-risk capital, to fund interventions that are on the "good" part of the scale, and suggest that early-stage equity capital be reserved for interventions that we determine are on the "best" side of the scale. Our aim in this approach is to ensure that best practices at least get a fighting chance to become industry standard. In the case of renewable energy, it meant supporting a later-stage investment in a microgrid company that was poised to scale rapidly—helping to prove the validity of microgrids—and seeking investments with more community ownership intrinsic to their models for the earlier-stage, higher-risk portfolio.

Put this all together, and this combination of strategies has helped build what I hope you'll agree is a pretty high-impact portfolio!

A lot of shareholder engagement work is about getting companies to share more information publicly—information about their carbon emissions, for example, or where they are spending their political donation dollars. In terms of impact, one could say that providing this sort of information is "good," but not "best"; it's a first step in moving companies to improve their practices, but it's a means rather than an end in itself.

Transparency is a tool of accountability, but it should not be confused with accountability itself. As I understand it, accountability means not just doing and disclosing what you think is right, but explaining your reasoning in a way that traces a clear line directly back to the values you claimed to promote.

Hence, as part our practice of accountability, we try to keep the website updated as much as possible, and I would encourage you to look there for the most accurate overview of Pi Investment's portfolio. Because portfolios are dynamic animals, I provide here just a high-level summary of where these investments have focused across asset classes, not naming particular names but giving a sense of sector and emphasis. I share this not as a model to emulate but rather simply to show the diversity of opportunities available in the growing field of impact investment.

DIRECT INVESTMENTS

For direct investments into private companies (think angel investments or venture capital), Pi's values are often best expressed, but not limited by, the following focus areas:

1. *Transitioning to a sustainable future.* Companies and strategies that enable a more inclusive transition to a clean energy economy. Typically we seek businesses

that democratize the ability to purchase, own or invest in clean energy, and/or encourage a shift in consumer behavior toward reduced consumption and an improved stewardship of resources.

2. *Reconnecting communities with sustainable, affordable and local food.* Companies and strategies specifically seeking to expand access to healthy and sustainable food, beyond the core of urban/affluent consumers that have been predominantly driving and benefiting from healthy food trends to date.

3. *Democratizing wealth.* Companies that encourage local innovation in enterprises that go beyond job creation to truly transform people's realities with respect to assets and power in society. A key areas of focus has been ethical supply chains, with an emphasis on transforming job quality and redefining the role of workers and suppliers as partners in governance and ownership.

4. *Organizing and advocacy.* Companies that help people come together toward common goals and build their capacity for collective action. We particularly emphasize online strategies that lead to or complement offline actions as well. We also look for companies that have the ability and desire to influence their industry through their public presence and voice.

We recognize that working effectively with early-stage social enterprises requires both flexibility and intentionality in structuring investments. Hence, direct investments range from debt to quasi-equity, revenue-based finance, and "traditional" venture equity. We also pay special attention in deal structuring to ensure the long-term mission of the enterprise.

PRIVATE DEBT FUNDS

Private debt funds are typically bucketed as a category of fixed income in that they aim to provide a predictable return over a certain period of time (generally, the longer you're willing to lock up funds, the more interest the fund will promise). The impact field is happily saturated with private debt funds across a very wide variety of themes.

Pi Investments has supported funds in the United States that invest in worker-owned cooperatives, help mobile home owners buy the land beneath them, and support small business in rural areas. Internationally, Pi has supported funds that finance agricultural cooperatives, and that promote the growth of independent media in countries with a history of media oppression.

PRIVATE EQUITY FUNDS

From seed-stage funds to venture capital to mezzanine and later-stage funds, there is also a great diversity of offerings for private equity funds in impact investment.

Pi has supported a number of funds that focus on serving low-income, diverse populations across the US, that are in turn managed by diverse fund managers who intimately understand their target markets. A number of others are focused on quality job creation, ideally through ventures that provide a socially/environmentally useful product in the process.

Currently, Pi has limited exposure to international funds, generally preferring to invest directly in companies on a selective basis. However, investing in international funds can be a great way for investors to get exposure to a very broad range of deal flow, and also to support the growth of impact investment ecosystems globally.

REAL ASSETS

Real assets, as the term implies, is an investment category largely entailing things you can touch—real estate, forestland and timber, precious metals or minerals, and so on. Because this category includes many renewable and nonrenewable resources, it is critical to first consider sector by sector what types of investments are appropriate in the first place, and then identify best practices in that particular sector. Also, because the exit/mechanism of financial return typically involves passing that asset to someone else (just as when you sell your house!), who the asset will be sold to and what they will do with it becomes a very critical question to address.

Pi has focused on investments in sustainably managed forestry and low-income housing. In this category Pi has also taken a closer look at fund-of-fund products, because a number of real asset funds have high minimum investment requirements compared to other asset classes, so it can be harder to get to a decent level of diversification.

Like all portfolios, this one is still a work in progress—my hope is that this chapter leaves you with some new strategies for how to implement a 100 percent portfolio with real, transformative impact, strategies that as a field we will continue to build upon and improve over time.

eleven

WHAT YOU CAN DO

C AN WE APPROACH THE WHOLE GLOBAL ECONOMY WITH A transformative framework? I would argue that it is possible to rebuild the economy from the ground up, and for individuals from all class backgrounds to be leaders in this transition.

Not all of us have access to a large portfolio of investments, of course. So what can the average person do? There are ways that everyone can participate in impact investment—by leveraging their connections to resources, no matter how big or small, by launching a project, or by holding impact investment accountable as it scales.

REAL IMPACT FOR EVERYDAY INVESTORS

Have you ever felt that icky feeling when you believe in certain values, but know that your money is supporting all the things you hate?

If you're reading this book, I presume you take your contribution to social and environmental change seriously. Maybe it's part of your day job, maybe it's in the way you carefully compost and recycle, take a reusable bag to the grocery store, go to protests, examine your role in racial justice, and in general try to have great intentionality around your everyday life decisions. Maybe you're even part of the impact investment industry, but focus your energy on managing other people's money.

And yet, despite your concern for social issues, I'll speculate that the investment portfolio you have now—whether it consists of a savings account at a big-name bank and a 401(k) invested in mutual funds, or trusts, stocks, bonds, college savings plans, a mortgage, or even credit debt—probably doesn't fit you right. This is not your fault; you're simply invested in the same things anyone else is who walks into a financial institution looking for guidance. The problem is that once you understand how your financial institution is using your money, the "ick factor" sinks in, and it's very hard to remove it from your awareness.

But not to fear—you can look forward to restful nights and ick-free days. The process of realigning your money with your values is really not that difficult.

Just move your money!

I have presented four simple steps below—each of which can be done in thirty minutes or less. So once you work up the will, you could be two hours away from an ick-free life. Some of them fit the guidelines of Transformative Finance—some, quite frankly, do not, but are still light-years ahead of conventional business practice, and your engagement could be part of what helps lead them toward even deeper impact over time.

These suggestions are intended to provide a purely educational overview of options available in the universe of social investment. It is not financial advice, and is not meant to endorse any particular product, service, or firm. Information on each institution and opportunity was taken from their individual websites and may have changed since the time of publication.

Personal financial management is, by nature, personal. Make good decisions for yourself in regard to your needs, impact interests, and tolerance for risk; ideally, you should connect with a professional financial advisor before pursuing any investments.

Step 1: Break Up with Your Bank

Chances are, your money is sitting at a big-name bank. Presumably, every time you call or walk in you have to go through eight security checks to get any transaction done, and every few months you're sure to get hit with some unexpected late fee or maintenance fee. And of course, your money is likely going to fund all sorts of terrible stuff.

The good news is that there are a number of community banks that can provide all the things you'd typically want—free checking and savings, free ATMs, depositing checks through your cell phone, all the bells and whistles—and most importantly, they are insured by the Federal Deposit Insurance Corporation (FDIC), meaning that your money is just as secure as it would be at a major bank, backed up by the federal government.

The banks listed in Table 4 have all the above services— and rates that are at least comparable to the (generally dismal) interest rates offered by conventional banks these days. They also have the perk that even if you have only a small amount of

TABLE 4. Community Bank Options

Name	Location	Impact Focus	Bells and Whistles
Amalgamated Bank	New York City	Union-owned bank; labor rights focused	Free access to 50,000 ATMs nationally; online bill pay and phone check deposit
Beneficial State Bank	Oakland, CA	Broad: community development, low-income housing, sustainable business, etc.	Free access to 50,000 ATMs; online bill pay and phone check deposit
Carver Bank	New York City	First African American and Caribbean American owned bank	Free access to 50,000 ATMs; online bill pay
New Resource Bank	San Francisco	Environment, local food, renewable energy	All ATM fees refunded, included globally; online bill pay and phone check deposit, retirement accounts
Self-Help Credit Union	North Carolina, California, Washington, DC	Emphasis on serving low-income communities with innovative products like special accounts for immigrants	Free access to 50,000 ATMs; online bill pay and phone check deposit, retirement accounts
Sunrise Bank	Minneapolis, St. Paul	Emphasis on serving low-income communities	Telebanking, retirement accounts

money, you'll typically still be assigned a good, old-fashioned *banker*—someone you can email or call directly without waiting on hold for half an hour listening to elevator music, who will literally know you by your first name.

So, in essence: better service, without the ick. It starts to feel like a pretty obvious choice.

Even if you don't live in one of these states, you can open an account. You'll need to sign and send in the first document, but after that, you don't really need to have any interaction with a branch if you don't want to—everything can be done online these days. If you prefer to find a community bank, credit union, or co-op in your local area, check out the Opportunity Finance Network (http://ofn.org/cdfi-locator) for listings.

What does it take to break up with your bank? It's actually pretty fun, and it takes about ten minutes. I had banked at a certain big-name bank since I was child, and I gave them a call a few years back. The conversation went like this:

BANK REPRESENTATIVE: What can I do for you today?

ME: I'd like to close my accounts.

BANK REPRESENTATIVE: Okay, ma'am, no problem, I can do that for you. Can you please tell me why? Can I convince you to stay?

ME: I am concerned your bank is supporting businesses that do terrible things like fracking, mining, and supporting human rights abuses. I don't want to be a part of that, so I'm moving my money to a community bank. Can you please write that down in the notes for your supervisor?

BANK REPRESENTATIVE: Um, oh. I can put that in my notes. Is there anything I can do to convince you to stay?

ME: Yes. Can the bank improve its social and environmental policies to be a better global citizen? If not, then I cannot continue to support it.

BANK REPRESENTATIVE: I'm sorry, ma'am. I can help you close the account. Where would you like me to send the check or wire?

ME: Please send it to my new account at my favorite community bank—account number xxxxx, routing number yyyyy.

BANK REPRESENTATIVE: Okay. This will be executed within forty-eight hours and your accounts will be closed.

I include the full actual conversation to show that, although the prospect of breaking up with your bank might seem intimidating, it's really that simple and quick. Add an extra twenty minutes or so to provide your new account number to any services you access or bills you pay via autopay, and the whole thing takes thirty minutes, tops.

I'll note that one major thing that community banks often *don't* do is provide mortgages. Before I broke up with my big-name bank, I called first to check and see if my having been a loyal customer would make a difference when it came time to buy a house. Would I be sacrificing any "relational capital" I had built?

And the sad thing in our crazy world of financial disintermediation is that I learned that twenty years of being a client with a perfect track record *makes ZERO difference* in your ability to access a mortgage, as your mortgage will be sold three times before you make your second payment anyway. So don't worry—you're not missing out on anything.

Step 2: Start Your Rainy-Day Fund

If you are financially prudent (and can afford it), you probably have some money in your savings account that you envision as a rainy-day fund—an amount equivalent to a few months of pay or rent in case of unexpected shifts in your life, or what you're saving for a wedding, home down payment, or other major life event—something that you don't intend to touch in the next year (or two or three).

With savings accounts offering less than 0.1 percent in interest these days, it can be worthwhile to put some money into a longer-term instrument, called a private debt fund, that could earn you 2 percent or more.[1] If you wind up having to take the money out early in an emergency, you'll typically just sacrifice some degree of interest—which, given how little you would have made at a bank, is not much of a risk—and you will not lose any of the original deposit in the process.

Most of these longer-term offerings come with some layer of philanthropic money from foundations serving as a guarantee against losses, similar to (though not quite as secure as) the way the FDIC protects banks. The organizations listed in Table 5 provide higher interest rates than a bank—for instance, at the time of writing, Bank of America offered a 0.07 percent return for a one-year investment with a $10,000 minimum—a rate *six times* lower than any of the opportunities listed in the table, which require minimum investments of as little as $20—making them the best-kept secrets in finance.[2] Even as interest rates inevitably shift in the future, these opportunities are likely to remain competitive. They also offer you the ability to direct that your money be used for a

TABLE 5. Fixed Income Options

Name	Impact Focus	Offerings (at the time of writing)
Calvert Foundation	Twelve different funds supporting women's empowerment, local business, education, affordable housing, fair trade, etc.	$20 minimum. Terms range from one to ten years with interest rates ranging from 0.5 to 3 percent annually and 100 percent repayment rate over the past twenty years.
Media Development Investment Fund	Supporting independent media in newly democratizing countries	$1,000 minimum. Terms range from one to ten years with interest rates of up to 3 percent annually and 100 percent repayment rate over the past eighteen years.
RSF Social Investment Fund	Supporting sustainable businesses, arts programs, and Waldorf schools	$1,000 minimum. Three-month term (i.e., you can keep your money in or take it out each quarter) with 0.25 percent interest rate (lower than the others because of the shorter term) and over 98 percent repayment rate over the past thirty years.

much more targeted impact, if there is a specific area of social change you want to support.

Table 5 presents just a sampling of the available options. You can also think about using these funds as a fun way to "gift" a college-fund contribution to a favorite niece or nephew rather than buying an old-fashioned savings bond.

To participate, you can usually just sign up online (it's as easy as checking out on Amazon). Again, this list is just a starting place—be sure to check out other debt funds on the market or ask your financial advisor for more information. It will take you, at most, thirty minutes to decide on your most exciting impact opportunity and send in your check!

Step 3: Clean Up Your Stocks

You may have stocks that you manage yourself through a platform like Fidelity, or you may be paying a financial manager at a firm like Morgan Stanley to make those choices. Often, they simply ask you if you're risk-level A, B, or C, and then provide extremely limited information about where your money is actually invested. As New Resource Bank, one of the banks listed in Table 4, points out on its website, you should "know where your money spends the night." If you don't—then presume it's not likely to be where you'd want it to be.[3]

Table 6 lists choices that you can simply invest in yourself; or you can provide this list as an educational example to your financial advisor, in addition to asking what social platforms his or her firm already offers. Once again, these are just a few of the many options available—from mutual funds to REITs to ETFs. (If you don't know what those are, don't worry—you can easily learn, and your financial advisor will be impressed. A REIT, or real estate investment trust, is a portfolio of real estate assets that is managed like a mutual fund; an ETF, or exchange-traded fund, tries to replicate the returns of a certain index, such as the NASDAQ. Essentially, what you need to know is that they function a lot like mutual funds for retail investors.)

Will you make less money? Multiple research studies say no.

In 2012, Deutsche Bank analyzed 100 academic studies on sustainable investing and concluded that companies with high environmental, social, and governance (ESG) ratings were

TABLE 6. Public Equity Options

Name	Ticker	Impact Focus
Pax World Global Environmental Markets	PGRNX	Mutual fund in sustainable food and agriculture, waste and water management, and energy
CRA (Community Reinvestment Act) Qualified Investment Fund	CRATX	Community-focused government bonds, such as affordable housing
Calvert Global Water Fund	CFWAX	Mutual fund in water infrastructure
PowerShares WilderHill Clean Energy Fund	PBW	Renewable energy (ETF)

financially outperforming the market over the medium or long term.[4] This finding was supported by a 2011 Harvard Business School study that examined 180 US firms in the 1990s and 2000s. The Harvard study grouped the companies into "high-sustainability" and "low-sustainability" cohorts and found that those that embedded strong sustainability policies in their strategies and operations outperformed their competitors by almost 4 percent a year. By the end of the eighteen-year study period, compounding growth resulted in the high-sustainability companies having market capitalizations that were almost double those of their low-sustainability competitors.

The authors attributed this outperformance to several factors, including more engaged workforces, more secure licenses to operate, more loyal and satisfied customer bases, better relationships with stakeholders, greater transparency, more collaborative communities, and better ability to innovate.[5] In addition to evidence of the financial outperformance of companies with higher ESG ratings, both studies also pointed to the risks mitigated by adopting effective practices with regards to health and safety, good governance, and climate change management, leading to lower share price volatility.

In general, of course, there are no guarantees on returns, mostly because, as we've seen time and again, it's easy to make or lose money in the stock market no matter what. For instance, people who divested from fossil fuels this past year dodged a bullet: a study commissioned by the Associated Press found that a $1 billion endowment that divested from fossil fuels would have saved a whopping $119 million, enough for 850 four-year scholarships.[6] But markets are always cyclical and multifaceted, so it's hard to put too much faith in such statements of causality.

Conventional wisdom would say proper diversification is probably more important than whether or not your funds take social and environmental values into account. And for those who have a long-term investment horizon, it's hard not to believe that the bad choices companies make now, such as overinvesting in nonrenewable resources, won't impact their returns in the long term. That's in part why major insurance companies, such as Swiss Re, and pension funds, including the New York City Employee Retirement System, have implemented environmental, social, and governance practices—not because of any social conscience, necessarily, but simply out of concern for their long-term viability.

Your financial advisor may respond by saying that investing in this way is a terrible idea, and that you'll lose money. Often this response comes from a place of fear of the unknown—the advisor doesn't have the expertise in social investment to feel confident making recommendations, and therefore shies away from it. He or she then has a choice to make—to either take a learning journey with you, or to risk losing a client.

If you have a truly resistant advisor, there are fortunately plenty of others out there who now have decades of experience incorporating their clients' values into their investments. You can obtain a list of socially oriented advisors across the country through the First Affirmative Financial Network.[7] As you can imagine, financial advisors who have chosen to dedicate their careers to social investing tend to be pretty cool people; you might wind up not only with a new financial advisor, but with a new friend.

Step 4: Retire in Style

Sadly, employer-provided retirement accounts are becoming rare, but if you're lucky, you may still have one.

If so, yours may offer a social impact investment fund option already (such as TIAA-CREF, for instance). But a variety of other social options could be added to an employer plan, such as Social(k) or Green Retirement, Inc. These can be great choices to recommend to your human resources manager—they are very cost-effective even for small organizations or nonprofits as a platform for retirement funds.

If your job doesn't offer a retirement plan, or you're an independent contractor, you may want to start an IRA or Roth IRA through your financial advisor or bank, which has major tax benefits. These retirement funds can be managed in a social fashion as well; you can open your account at one of the social banks listed above, or simply ask your financial advisor to explore social and environmental options.

How do you start a retirement fund? It's a lot easier than you might imagine—and definitely can be done in under twenty minutes. If you have an accountant, call and ask what kind of account he or she would recommend for you—IRA, Roth IRA, or SEP IRA. You'll likely be well-served by going with what the accountant says, as he or she is already familiar with your tax situation. If you do not have an accountant, you will need to do some more research. But here is a quick overview.

With a traditional IRA, savings are not taxed in the year you make the deposit, and you don't pay any tax until you reach retirement age and take the money out (at that point, presumably your effective tax rate will be lower as your overall income is lower, so you'll get to keep more of the money). With a Roth IRA, savings are taxed in the year you make the deposit, but *not* when you take the money out. If you are self-employed or a small business owner, you can also opt for a SEP IRA. A SEP IRA follows most of the same rules as a traditional IRA, and will not be taxed until withdrawals are made. However, it is easier and less expensive for businesses to set up than a 401(k) plan. Its funding flexibility is also a draw, allowing you to skip contributions during years when business is down and contribute as much as 25 percent of your net income or $53,000 (whichever is less) in better years.

In general, think that for every $5,000 you're able to save, depending on your effective tax rate, you can get roughly $1,000 "free" from the government to pay for a few extra margaritas on the beach. The question is, do you want those margaritas now, or when you retire? What is best or possible for you is very specific to your personal financial situation and tax bracket, so do be sure to check in with your accountant.[8]

FROM INDIVIDUAL ACTION TO SYSTEMIC CHANGE

Moving your own money is a great thing to do, although, depending on the size of your bank account, it may feel like a largely symbolic action, like recycling. Arguably, such individual efforts *do* eventually make a collective difference. They are not to be ignored, especially when they are so easy to do. However, many people want to influence economic change in a bigger way, beyond their personal resources.

There are two main pathways for activists and aspiring change makers to take if they want to leverage the tools of impact investment for systemic change:

» *Starting profit-generating enterprises:* Activists can start enterprises that provide earned income for their organization in order to lessen its dependency on philanthropy, or in a way that they believe reflects how the economy should work, such as by setting up a worker-owned co-op.
» *Holding investments accountable:* There are a number of strategies to influence investments that are not fulfilling their social or environmental duties to society, whether they are traditional investments or impact-oriented investments and enterprises that may have gone astray.

Each of these activities merits a whole book on its own; here I will just provide an overview of the opportunities and resources available to people who seek to go in one of these directions.

Starting Profit-Generating Enterprises

For many people engaged in movement-building activities like organizing, political advocacy, or direct action, the idea of starting a profit-generating enterprise may feel like a radical departure. Even if we don't love it, a lot of us have gotten used to raising philanthropic dollars as a necessary distraction from doing the work itself. So why do something even more time consuming and complex? There are both a moral argument and a practical argument to support this.

The moral argument goes back to the story about the Gates Foundation, which was investing twice as much money in oil companies that were causing health problems in Nigeria as it was in health-care interventions, which meant essentially that it was profiting off of the problem, in the name of funding the solution. Many nonprofit organizations or movement entities won't take money from corporations based on the concept of conflict of interest, but to some degree, accepting funds from a foundation that is invested in the same companies is just one step removed from also participating in the spoils of the problem you're trying to solve.

Where to draw the line about what money you will and won't accept is a question with different answers for diverse organizations and communities, and it's impossible to set a hard and fast rule. At the Responsible Endowments Coalition, our line was that we would not take a donation from anyone we would ever consider campaigning against (which actually led to us turning down six-figure checks on two occasions). We did, however, take money from foundations, knowing that some had been started with funds garnered in fairly nefarious ways or had investments in entities we didn't like—though many of them were active participants in impact investment, of course. We earned only a limited amount of income from our conferences and events and thus predominantly relied on philanthropy to fill out our budget; we didn't see any other way of sustaining ourselves. In general we felt comfortable with the idea that *all* money, given that it's circulating in the current global economy, which has been built on unsustainable principles and practices, is, to some degree, dirty. Now that such wealth exists in the world, we would rather see it go toward radical social change than not. But ultimately—and as we have tried to do in the context of Transform Finance, which seeks to raise a third of its budget from earned revenue—the "cleanest" money one can find is that which we make ourselves through activities aligned with our values.

The practical argument is the more compelling and urgent one. As noted in Chapter 1, philanthropy is simply a drop in the bucket of the global economy, and it will never be able to provide enough resources to rebuild the economy at large enough scale to engage in a fair fight against entrenched interests.

The good news is that many foundations are beginning to recognize the discrepancy between their investments and their broader purpose, and many exemplary institutions, such as the Heron Foundation, the Wallace Global Fund, and the Packard Foundation, have worked hard to align their portfolios with their mission statements. As foundations reassess where they invest, an interesting opportunity has arisen for activist groups to access much larger checks. While an average grant might be $75,000, a starting investment might be $250,000, or in the millions, depending on the asset class. This investment action serves both practical and moral goals, since those investment dollars may previously have been allocated to enterprises and institutions with little interest in global economic transformation.

In response to these two trends—the relatively small pool of foundation funding available for social justice work, and the new opportunities emerging to access impact investment dollars—organizations have been innovating models to support themselves through earned income and related enterprises. A few examples worth noting:

» *Homeboy Industries:* Homeboy Industries in Los Angeles provides former gang members a place to learn job skills and work in one of its established social enterprises. The enterprises include a bakery, a farmer's market, and a catering service. Although Homeboy receives funding from a cross-section of private foundations, board members, and other donors, the revenue gained from its social enterprises covers 25 percent of the costs needed to sustain all of its free (and paying!) programs and services for its community. As the founder, Father Greg Boyle, a Catholic Jesuit priest, is fond of saying, "We don't hire homies to bake bread. We bake bread to hire homies."[9]

» *National Domestic Workers Alliance (NDWA):* NDWA is a network of nannies, housekeepers, and care workers that works for the respect, recognition, and inclusion in labor protection for domestic workers. With more than sixty affiliate organizations, the NDWA leads several national and international initiatives focusing on labor protection advocacy, grassroots innovation, and immigration and trafficking. Faircare Labs, one of NDWA's initiatives, seeks to raise market norms in the domestic-work sector through testing and incubating innovative business models that have the potential to disrupt exploitative care markets while generating revenue for NDWA.[10]

» *Restaurant Opportunities Centers (ROC):* ROC is a national workers' center founded in 2002 dedicated to improving working conditions in the restaurant industry. Its 25,000-plus worker-members across fifteen states advocate for policy changes like the elimination of the tipped minimum wage (only $2.13 nationally—as it has been for a hundred years!); they also receive access to training to help them advance their careers in the restaurant industry. ROC has opened two restaurants, in New York and Detroit, and has plans to expand next to New Orleans and Oakland. These restaurants serve as model employers, provide valuable training to workers, and also provide revenue to the non-profit itself to help achieve sustainability over time.[11]

» *National Association for Latino Community Asset Builders (NALCAB):* NALCAB is a network of more than one hundred nonprofit community-development and asset-building organizations serving low- and moderate-income communities. Its members focus on implementing market-based strategies for creating jobs, developing neighborhood assets, and building family wealth. They do so by working on an array of issues, such as affordable housing, micro-lending, and economic development. In 2016, the organization launched a fund with the aim of producing and preserving affordable housing in largely Latino communities, especially in areas that are experiencing rapid appreciation or gentrification. This effort, which is being implemented in collaboration with NALCAB's members, takes advantage of the relationships that these members have been building with their communities over decades. Its goal is to create a highly accountable structure to place capital and to assist in assuring the overall sustainability of the NALCAB network.[12]

In all of these cases, the enterprises themselves serve the beneficiary community while *also* building revenue for the nonprofit organization itself. That approach can be game changing. Imagine, as an executive director, that 50 percent of the time you spend fundraising that would have previously taken you away from your community is now spent on providing your community with a useful service. And that your organization would have just as much if not more money than it did before, without you having to raise it. How much further could you get toward your mission?

As this idea has become more popular, an interesting array of organizations have emerged to support movement leaders interested in exploring earned revenue models:

» *Transform Finance* hosts the Transform Finance Institute for Social Justice Leaders both domestically and internationally, a multiday workshop that introduces leaders to impact investment, both from the perspective of launching projects and from that of holding impact investment accountable.[13]

» *Accelerate Change* supports institutions seeking to scale by helping them develop innovative member benefits that would be of value to the people they seek to organize, leading them to be financially sustainable (think AAA, but for progressive movements).[14]

» *The Workers Lab* provides financial resources, training, and technical assistance to community organizers and entrepreneurs working toward a dignified labor market. One of its goals in doing so is to help them build self-sufficient revenue models that can sustain themselves for the long run.[15]

Foundations have also been increasingly interested in funding experiments by established social justice organizations to pursue more effective earned-income strategies—so it may be worth approaching historical funders to see about their supporting such an experiment or planning period.

Another reason for starting an enterprise is to build a successful economic model that can challenge the dominant economic paradigm. Activists are often criticized for being great at saying no to existing structures without offering viable alternatives. Building an enterprise is a great opportunity to be equal parts lover and fighter: helping people in the short term, through the enterprise, while also fighting back against broader economic trends.

What does this mean in practice? It means different things to different organizations. It might mean a renters' rights organization seeking to build community land trusts. Or a day-laborer association starting a cooperative. Or a women's empowerment group starting a day-care center. In general, as you consider these examples, I'd invite you to think about the ways that you're currently fighting against an entrenched system, and what loving alternative you might be able to provide.

For some organizations, loving and fighting simultaneously is already deep within their DNA. And some, who may be faced with an urgent crisis to fight back against (such as an impending land grab), may not feel they have the time or resources to invest in developing new projects, since they need to marshal all their energy to defend what they already have. Once again, there is no one correct approach. My invitation to you here is just to consider to what degree your movement currently balances loving and fighting. Does this balance feel right to you, and to your constituents?

Finally, for those who are looking to start a project, it's important to note that you don't need to run back to school for an MBA! There are resources for aspiring entrepreneurs to access training, mentorship, and start-up funding. Some of these do not charge an upfront fee, but may ask for equity. As noted previously, the field could use a more robust infrastructure to support aspiring entrepreneurs coming from the social sector—but at least there are a few high-quality programs available for those ready to dive in. Here are some examples:

» *Uncharted Institute:* The Uncharted Institute is a program that unites entrepreneurs with the potential to address major problems at scale. By connecting entrepreneurs with mentors, investors, and fellow entrepreneurs, Uncharted aims to better position them to tackle social and environmental problems. Besides hosting three five-week accelerator programs each year—in the United States, Mexico, and Uganda—Uncharted has launched dozens of labs around the world that deliver five-day programs for entrepreneurs, coupled with support before and long after the program ends.[16]

» *Global Social Benefit Institute (GSBI):* GSBI serves social entrepreneurs who are attempting to develop innovative, sustainable pathways out of poverty. It offers a three-day workshop for early-stage entrepreneurs, an online program for entrepreneurs in the validation stage, and a ten-month program for established social entrepreneurs who are looking to massively scale their solutions. The accelerator program is followed by an investor showcase where entrepreneurs present their work to Silicon Valley investors and donors. All programs have an extensive mentorship component that takes advantage of the GSBI's broad network.[17]

» *Village Capital:* Village Capital finds, trains, and funds entrepreneurs solving global problems. It operates business development programs for early-stage entrepreneurs in agriculture, education, energy, financial inclusion, and health. VilCap Investments, its affiliated, for-profit investment fund, invests in the two top-ranked graduates from each program. Its model relies on a peer-selection process whereby, after each program workshop, the entrepreneurs rank each other against a series of set criteria. The entrepreneurs with the top rankings receive over $50,000 in investment.[18]

» *SMASHD Labs:* This is a ten-week accelerator program in Los Angeles led by legendary angel investor Troy Carter and the multidisciplinary team at Atom Factory, a brand-management company known for hits like Lady Gaga and John Legend. They focus on early-stage companies at the intersection of culture and technology. Participating companies benefit from the Atom Factory's expertise in branding and marketing as well as its extensive network. The program is also a great way to spend quality time with Cross Culture Ventures, a fund cofounded by Troy Carter and Marlon Nichols.[19]

Holding Investments Accountable

As billions of dollars move into impact investments, it's important for activists to also pay attention to the projects currently under development and to take advantage of leverage points available to enhance their impact. Whether addressing impact or non-impact companies and projects, there are three main entry points into the accountability conversation:

» *Shareholder activism:* Shareholder activism can be a very effective way of promoting change within major corporations, as noted in my example in Chapter 2 about Lockheed Martin. Organizations like As You Sow and the Interfaith Center on Corporate Responsibility can be great ones to partner up with—they have deep expertise and are happy to work with advocacy groups.

» *Investment accountability work:* Investments will always have some kind of social or environmental impact, whether positive or negative. Investors need to be held accountable when their best intentions fail (or their lack of intention causes harm). Some of this work will come quite naturally to groups already used to looking at projects funded by the World Bank and other global institutions. I would just encourage these groups to expand their scope to consider impact investments, too. For instance, the International Accountability Project has done fantastic work assembling global leadership councils of affected communities, then arranging for them to meet with investment institutions to hold them accountable for their impact.[20]

» *Community integration efforts:* When investment projects are already in the works, one tactic is to ensure that a certain level of community integration and accountability is established, typically in the form of a "community benefit agreement." I hesitate to use that term, as it implies that community benefit should be an "add on" rather than something that is integral to the work of a business or investment. However, the community benefit agreement model is one that can be adapted, ideally to extend beyond a onetime arrangement, to set the terms for ongoing community participation in the design, governance, and ownership of an intervention. The first community benefit agreement, for example, completed in New York in 2005, was established in relation to the million-dollar Atlantic Yards arena project. The arena, which was meant to be the home of the New Jersey Nets (to be renamed the Brooklyn Nets), was met with broad opposition from Brooklyn residents. Community groups organized and negotiated the agreement, focusing on affordable housing, a living wage, local and equitable hiring provisions, a commitment to build a day-care center, and the perk of free basketball tickets for neighborhood residents.[21]

I hope the stories of these pioneering organizations and initiatives help to confirm my message from back in Chapter 1: that we are *all* connected to money in one way or another, and therefore have the ability to affect how it works in society. Whether as an individual; as a member of a community-based organization, nonprofit, or social movement; or as part of an investment institution, perhaps one or more of the options above will inspire you to be a more powerful activist and advocate.

CONCLUSION

Asking Questions

I AM HIGHLY OPTIMISTIC ABOUT IMPACT INVESTMENT'S potential to have a transformative effect on the massive social and environmental challenges of our time. We have the opportunity to leverage trillions of dollars for justice. That is truly amazing! We may or may not ultimately take adequate advantage of such an opportunity, but I do hope that this book has succeeded in giving you a clear sense that finance can be an incredibly effective tool for social change.

The sobering reality is that the path ahead of us is a long one, if we want to turn these ideas and values into actual social transformation. To share a favorite quote from E. B. White that generally reflects my outlook on life: "If the world were merely seductive, that would be easy. If it were merely challenging, that would be no problem. But I arise in the morning torn between a desire to improve the world and a desire to enjoy the world. This makes it hard to plan the day."[1]

Deep down, sometimes I still have to ask myself: How did the world get so screwed up? How did we wind up with methods of social and economic organization that destroy us rather than serve us? Why do we, at a societal level, just let this happen? Why do we need to spend our time fighting for justice when there are so many other amazing ways to spend it? These questions perplex me and break my heart over and over again.

We may be keenly aware of the cumulative consequences of our decisions and actions, and even perturbed by them, but we may also feel that our individual choices about our modest bank accounts, or the products we buy, can't change much in a world driven by financial interests rather than by human needs and moral values. Even those who have access to significant resources, whether via institutions or personal wealth, may still feel as though their influence is just a drop in the bucket.

The billions of people worldwide whose social, political, cultural, and economic autonomy has been jeopardized by the global economy are painfully aware of the injustice and inequity it has perpetuated. They may not realize there are roads to economic development and greater prosperity other than the ones we've been taking, or may not recognize that they, too, have access to the economic power that can change the world.

Impact investment can harness this economic power and turn it into a force for good. We don't know if the impact investment field will ultimately choose to create new roads to prosperity for all, or stop short at making change on the margins. The good news is that we are still in the early days of impact investment, and while we may never achieve perfection, we have the opportunity to get some things right if we think very carefully about just what we are scaling, how, and for whom.

At the end of the day, this is my advice to you: Take advantage of every opportunity to work for justice, with every dollar, every word, every action. Listen. And keep asking questions.

ACKNOWLEDGMENTS

SOCIAL CHANGE WORK IS OFTEN CONSIDERED TO BE A LA-bor of love. I think of this from two primary perspectives: first, the love for ideas, the need to both wrestle with them and stand firm behind them; and second, the love for people, both humanity at large and the specific people we work alongside and try to man-ifest our values with in every moment.

In the process of curating and forming the ideas for this book and making it a reality, I have for many years been the recipient of love and generosity that leaves me feeling deeply fulfilled and overwhelmed with gratitude. Please know that behind every name listed below is an intense appreciation of the love I have witnessed each of you manifest, not only in your support of me and my daily well-being, but in your dedication to social justice.

Thank you to the people whose work both inspired and deepened the idea of Transform Finance:

To Sergio Oceransky, who first taught me that impact invest-ment could be something different and forced me to reconcile my desire to do more: you are one of the most generous spirits I've ever known and a true gift to the world.

To Brendan Martin, who has inspired generations of activists to see the transformative potential of finance done right: I'm grateful to have you as a caring friend and role model.

To Emily Stone, the mastermind behind Uncommon Cacao, who balances theory and practice in her work with a rigor, dedication, and joy that is unparalleled.

To Allison Basile, Deepti Doshi, Joanna Levitt, Mohamed Mongy, and Boa Monjane, who made important early contributions to the ideas behind Transform Finance, and whose support gave me the courage to continue pursuing it: you were all so open and giving, and continue to remind me how we can grow together in our commitment to activism.

To Rajasvini Bhansali, Shawn Escoffery, and Chid Liberty, board members of Transform Finance: your thoughtfulness and commitment to moving the vision forward have been an inspiration.

And finally, to the one and only Andrea Armeni, cofounder of Transform Finance, who has led the organization so elegantly as executive director: I know no one else so committed in equal measure to changing the world and to being a good person every day. I am so lucky to know you.

Thank you to the people who made me a better activist:
This book is dedicated to Janet Shenk, whose dedication to developing leaders, in the context of her overall support of movement building, is truly extraordinary. For many years I felt oddly as if I could never thank Janet enough, as if an unpaid debt were hanging over me. I had trouble articulating my gratitude as I was unable to put my finger on what exactly I was so grateful for; why Janet's role in my life was so deeply imprinted on my psyche. Recently I realized that beyond any particular action she took (though there are many), what made such a difference was the simple fact that

Janet believed in me so fiercely that she taught me to believe in myself. Thank you, Janet, for helping me recognize and step into my power, allowing me to embrace both my strength and imperfections. Your support has become a model for me in how to show up in relationship to others, especially for new leaders who similarly struggle to find the confidence it takes to take risks and build something new.

To Diana Cohn, who worked with Janet for many years and is still the fearless leader of the Panta Rhea Foundation, and has also been an incredible champion for our work for over a decade: I am grateful to count you as my friend and colleague. Diana was the first to jump in and support the book process, giving me more confidence to proceed than I'm sure she realized.

To Majora Carter and James Chase, who generously opened their home to me for many years and made huge contributions to my mental health as I slowly but surely learned how to be an executive director: your commitment to doing what's right has been incredibly inspiring, and I continue to learn so much from you both.

To Sibley Verbeck Simon, who has a deep commitment to justice: your willingness to take visionary, risky steps in both supporting and founding new initiatives is extraordinary.

To Van Jones, who was so generous in supporting a young organization for no other reason than that he believed in it, serving as a mentor to me and to so many others, and who always went the extra mile to support us—often quite literally (for instance, he once took a redeye to Atlanta and back just to speak to a group of HBCU students for the Responsible Endowments Coalition): your sharp analysis and ability to capture the world's attention, combined with a strong commitment to values, have been exemplary.

To Kesha Cash, who has helped me to be smarter and clearer in my ideas: your friendship has nourished me time and time again, and your energy inspires me to get to work.

Thank you to the people who opened up the world of impact investment to me—and have supported me in pushing it forward:

To Diane Bratcher, who helped me file that first shareholder resolution at Lockheed Martin, and who was so generous with her time and support when a nineteen-year-old walked into her office in the "G–d Box" in New York City; and to Shelley Alpern, who similarly supported our early efforts at the Responsible Endowments Coalition: both of you, alongside so many other industry powerhouses, such as Tim Smith and Peter Kinder, empowered us with your encouragement.

To Cheyenna Weber, who first introduced me to the concept of co-ops and plunged her heart and soul into the students of the Responsible Endowments Coalition; and to Dan Apfel and Marcie Smith, keepers of the flame: all of you have brought admirable intelligence and graciousness to the organization.

To my cofounders at Toniic, Sean Foote, Lisa and Charly Kleissner, and John Kohler, and to Stephanie Cohn-Rupp, Adam Bendell, and Alison Grant, who have demonstrated continuing stewardship and commitment to impact: thank you for all your leadership.

To Tal Pritzker and Choresh Wald, who have shown exceptional trust, wisdom, courage, and commitment to values: I learn so much from both of you, and our work together has been truly life-changing. Many thanks as well to Mary Parthe, Michelle Nakfoor, Evangelia Liaskas, and John Ringer for their important roles in this journey.

To Regan Pritzker and the exceptional teams at TAO Capital and the Libra Foundation: I greatly value your leadership, creativity in impact, and incredible openness and support.

And to Aner Ben-Ami, my business partner: I can't even imagine where I would be without your steady hand, thoughtfulness, understanding, and support. This book is as much yours as mine, given what we have built together, and I couldn't ask for a better partner in this work.

Thank you to the people who made this book come to life:

To Sasha Abramsky, *New York Times* best-selling author, without whose encouragement there literally would be no book (after a whirlwind five days of writing on the beach in Brazil, I sent him a first draft and said, "If this is terrible, tell me now and I'll stop. . . . If it's good then you have to help me"): I'm so glad you liked it—and consequently, so graciously and freely gave of your time and expertise in support of the project.

My sincere thanks to the many, many individuals who supported the crowdfunding campaign for the book, which enabled me to bring on the editor of my dreams, Lisa Kaufman. To Debra Schwartz, Jen Astone, and Ellen Friedman, a trio of powerful women I am blessed to consider both colleagues and friends, who helped facilitate critical support that in turn ensured this book would make it into the universe. Special thanks in particular to Shelley Alpern, Aner Ben-Ami, Adam Bendell, Suzanne Biegel, Diana Cohn, John Fullerton, Alison Grant, Kay and Jack Grossman, Kristin Hull, Wahleah Johns and Billy Parish, Jennifer Kassan, Danny Kennedy, Joshua Knauer, Pier LaFarge, Shawn Lesser, Ali Long, Josh Mailman, Diana Simon and Don Tringali, John Simon, Sarina Simon, Kiki Tidwell, Tabreez Verjee, and Michael Whelchel.

To Dylan Schneider and Nada Wahba, whose dedication to every detail of *Real Impact* made a huge difference in both getting the book out to the world and keeping my spirits high: I think you know how much I mean it when I say I could not have done this without you.

To Victoria Skurnick and Jim Levine of LGR Literary, agents who took a chance on an unknown author: your support, and good humor, were great additions to the process.

To Alessandra Bastagli, Katy O'Donnell, and the talented team at Nation Books, who similarly were open to working with a new author: you provided an exceptional level of guidance and support.

To Jessica Krakoski and Barbara Henricks of Cave Henricks, incredibly dedicated and principled publicists who likely had a hand in ensuring that this book got into your hands.

To Hannibal Abera, Jen Astone, Rajasvini Bhasali, Kesha Cash, Tom Chi, Steve Coleman, Claiborne Deming, Justina Lai, Joanna Levitt, Christine Looney, Luis Martinelli, Laura Ortiz, James Rucker, June Sale, Diana Simon, Mitchell Strauss, Don Tringali, Tabreez Verjee, and Shu Dar Yao: your painstaking reviews of early drafts led to a much improved manuscript.

And to Lisa Kaufman, my secret weapon, who is an incredible editor: you helped me not only sound like my best self, but forced me to really justify my arguments. If any readers get the chance, hire her in a heartbeat.

Thank you to the people who safeguard my spirit:

To my community of "artivists"—musicians and dancers who are deeply committed to supporting one another, whether through the spaces we create for beauty, creativity, and joy manifested on-stage or in the backstage moments of laughter: you all make me a better person.

To Carolyn Brandy, Elena De Troya, Allison Hammond, Jules Hilson, Vanessa Lindberg, Mena Ramos, and Elizabeth Sawyer: for your sisterhood, mentorship, and amazing playing; and to Royland Lovato, Vladimir Cepeda, Joe Churchill, Glendis Perez Villalon, Gustavo Ramos, Alan Rivera, and Angel Yoel Mulen: you are *familia* to me, and your warmth and support have been invaluable.

To all my teachers—Susana Arenas, Jose Francisco Barroso, Temistocles Betancourt, R. Charles, Zulema Pedroso Hardy, Lazaro Pedroso, Youssouf Koumbassa, Alhassane Camara, Aziz Faye, Babacar M'Baye, Joaquin Escamilla, Shane Sparks, Chebar Williams, Tovaris Wilson, Andre Fuentes, among so many others, and especially Felix Pupy Insua, Ibaye, the freest spirit I've ever met.

To the house dance community—Rama Hall, Junius Lee Brickhouse, Lauren Benjamin, Dana Fitchett, Nicole Klaymoon, Cody "Co-Flo" Ferreira, Tony McGregor, Mark Sanchez, Caleaf Sellers, and so many others who have served as teachers and community builders: you have always inspired me to imagine that there's more out there than what our current reality tells us, and then actually create it.

To the *capoeira* family—Professor Chipa and Monitora Beleza of Ginga Mundo Oakland; Mestre Sabia and Professor Tucano of Ginga Mundo in Salvador; Mestre Duzentos, Professor Ninho and Professor Sem Coluna of Grupo Senzala in Rio de Janèiro: thank you all for welcoming me with warm arms, and to so many others in the *capoeira* community who have been models in positive reinforcement and mutual support. *Muito obrigada, y muito axé!*

To Tatiana Campos, Iran Dos Santos, Kety Kim, Tiago Magalhães, Amar Mansoor, Rio Maracatu, Mario Pam, Fabio Sacramento, and so many others in Brazil, where the majority of this book was written: thank you for the incredibly warm welcome into your community and for sharing all your artistry.

To my incredible community of friends and mentors, whose encouragement and support played a tremendous part in this journey, including Nwamaka Agbo, Malena Amusa, Cherine Badawi, Denique Boxhill, Bruce Campbell, Amber Carrillo, Roberto Rojas Capo, Troy Carter, Ozbe Ceja, Isabel Clerie, Steve Colman, Cheryl Contee, Wanda Cuesta, Daryn Dodson, Yolanda Dorador, Sarah Farzam, Adrian Fenty, Sean Foster, Aisha Fukushima, Jessica Fyles, Leticia Gasca, Delonte Gholston, Mark Gonzales, Mark Hanis, Zakiya Harris, Gregory Hodge, Soraya Hosni, Sulaiman Hyatt, Saru Jayaranman, Wahleah Johns, Lucian Kahn, Sarah Kirnon, Pier La-Farge, Dana Lanza, Chid Liberty, Roberto Lovato, Javier Machado, Konda Mason, Achille Massoma, Matt Nelson, Jerry Nemorin, Fasica Netanyahu, Marlon Nichols, Steve O'Connell, Temi Ogunyoku, Jo Opot, Billy Parish, Jay Pugao, Mena Ramos, Ben Rattray, Adrian

Richardson, Nick Richetta, Favianna Rodriguez, James Rucker, D'Artagnan Scorza, Andre Leonardo dos Santos, Ken Sharpe, Daria Siciliano, Michael Sidgmore, Iris Smith, Rafael Smith, Michael Staton, Dan Stringer, John Sullivan, Folarin Tallman, Robert Terenzi, Pandora Thomas, Trevor Thomas, Luca Torre, Arely Villegas, Erin Wade, Mariam Wakili, Meg Watt, William Winters, Hana Yang, Biseat Yawkal, and Julie Yick, Nate Yohannes, Erina Williams: you are all, individually and collectively, the best. To Virginia Victoria Martinez: *mi madre Cubana, te quiero mucho.* And finally, to Priya Haji, a brilliant leader taken from us too soon: thank you, Priya, for all your support.

Thank you to the people I couldn't live without:

To my incredible family: I don't take a step in life without your guidance and unconditional love, and I am blessed to have you.

To Nina Simon: I admire you tremendously, and am so proud every time I get to say, "Yes, that's my sister." Thank you for all your love and support. I share this admiration and appreciation for her husband, Sibley Verbeck Simon, and daughter, Rocket Mo Simon.

To my father and favorite rockstar, Scott Simon: to you I owe my creativity, humor, storytelling, and love of people. My heart is fuller thanks to you. His wife, and my stepmother, Debbie Richetta Simon, has been an integral part of my life: thank you for all your support of my activism for so many years.

And to my mother, Sarina Simon: I am stronger every day because of you, kinder and more generous, more thoughtful, effective, and joyful. Your support is so much a part of me that any story of mine is yours as well.

ABOUT TRANSFORM FINANCE

TRANSFORM FINANCE AIMS TO TURN CAPITAL INTO A FORCE for transformative social change by building a bridge between the worlds of social justice and finance. Following the principles explained in *Real Impact*, we aim to support, inform, and organize investors and activists through advocacy, thought leadership, and advisory services.

HOW TO GET INVOLVED

There are currently three concrete ways to engage with Transform Finance (although we are always open to more ideas for how we can support your journey into impact!):

* *Investors and institutions* such as family offices and foundations are welcome to join the Transform Finance Investor Network, which launched at the White House in 2014 and has grown to over $2 billion in commitments. The members of this network meet monthly to deepen their investment practice in accordance with social justice values. Transform Finance can also provide

individual consulting and support to investor members on areas like impact thesis development and management, portfolio strategy, and diligence.

Activists and nonprofit leaders are welcome to join Transform Finance's trainings and institutes, both in the United States and overseas, which provide a comprehensive overview of impact investment practices, looking at how groups can create earned revenue opportunities and hold impact investments accountable. Attending institutions have included the National Domestic Workers Alliance, the Restaurant Opportunities Centers United (ROC), the Ella Baker Center, and the International Accountability Project, among others, and over 80 percent of the attendees in the United States have been people of color. In addition to these flagship trainings, Transform Finance can create customized content for foundations that want to empower their grantees around earned revenue and the interconnection of their work with the world of finance, as well as for activists working in a particular issue area or geographical region.

Social entrepreneurs, whether in an academic or incubator setting, can access content from Transform Finance to add a community-organizing and accountability lens to their standard curriculum and learn about alternative funding structures that are consistent with their missions. Content is available in English, Spanish, French, and Portuguese.

Updated information regarding ongoing activities can be found at www.transformfinance.org.

NOTES

CHAPTER 1: THE LIMITS OF CHARITY

1. P. L. Rosenfield, *A World of Giving: Carnegie Corporation of New York—A Century of International Philanthropy* (New York: PublicAffairs, 2014); D. Farrell, S. Lund, O. Skau, C. Atkins, J. Mengeringhaus, and M. Pierce, *Mapping Global Capital Markets: Fifth Annual Report*, McKinsey Global Institute, 2008.

2. The Foundation Center, *Social Justice Grantmaking 2: Highlights* (New York: The Foundation Center, 2009).

3. *Internal Revenue Manual*, Internal Revenue Service, 2016, https://goo.gl/XdwwDr, accessed June 3, 2016.

4. C. Piller, E. Sanders, and R. Dixon, "Dark Cloud over Good Works of Gates Foundation," *Los Angeles Times*, January 7, 2007.

5. R. J. Samuelson, "It's Still the Economy, Stupid," *Washington Post*, February 3, 2016.

CHAPTER 2: ECONOMIC ACTIVISM AND IMPACT INVESTMENT

1. "Finance and Investment Offices," Swarthmore College, n.d., http://goo.gl/YqEuVU, accessed February 2, 2017.

2. "Investments," California Public Employees' Retirement System (CalPERS), n.d., https://goo.gl/TIB9ea, accessed June 4, 2016; M. Braun,

"NYC Pension Weighs Liquidating $1.5 Billion Hedge Fund Portfolio," Bloomberg, April 13, 2016.

3. M. Hilton, ed., *Monitoring International Labor Standards: Quality of Information* (Washington, DC: National Academies Press, 2003).

4. T. Krattenmaker, "Swarthmore Presses Ahead with Lockheed Challenge Following Shareholder Vote," *Newswise*, May 7, 2002; J. Loviglio, "Swarthmore Challenges Lockheed Martin Discrimination Policy," Associated Press, April 1, 2002.

5. K. Downey, "Lockheed Changes Policy to Benefit Gays," *Washington Post*, November 23, 2002.

6. "Shareholder Resolution History," Walden Asset Management, 2016, http://goo.gl/weM28k, accessed June 4, 2016; Chris Bull, "Students vs. Big Business: A Swarthmore College Sophomore Talks About How Her Group Got the School to Use Its Economic Clout to Push for Gay Rights at Lockheed," *The Advocate*, May 14, 2002, 20, http://goo.gl/n3RWgg, accessed January 20, 2017.

7. Responsible Endowments Coalition, "New Coalition to Scrutinize College Investments," Corporate Social Responsibility Newswire, April 21, 2004, http://goo.gl/zOGBql.

8. "Innovative Finance," Rockefeller Foundation, n.d., https://goo.gl /mZ344r, accessed June 4, 2016.

9. "Impact Investing and Innovative Finance," Rockefeller Foundation, n.d., http://goo.gl/ahFt3x, accessed February 2, 2017.

10. D. Lamson, "Abolition," West Hills Friends, 2012, http://goo.gl /gFUwnR.

11. B. Upbin, "Impact Capital Is the New Asset Class," *Forbes*, September 18, 2012.

12. C. Tolentino, R. Sun, J. Cariola, X. Liu, and R. Gao, *Capstone Report* (New York: School of International and Public Affairs, Columbia University, 2015).

13. J. Matthews and D. Sternlicht, "Introducing the Impact Investing Benchmark." Cambridge Associates, Global Impact Investing Network, June 2015, http://goo.gl/NRs7GC, accessed January 20, 2017.

14. W. Cascio, "The High Cost of Low Wages," *Harvard Business Review*, December 2006.

15. D. Mulcahy, B. Weeks, and H. Bradley, *"We Have Met the Enemy . . . and He Is Us": Lessons from Twenty Years of the Kauffman Foundation's Investments in Venture Capital Funds and the Triumph of Hope over Experience*, Ewing Marion Kauffman Foundation, May 2012, http://goo.gl /UM1bK, accessed January 20, 2017.

16. Myles Udland, "Warren Buffett Thinks Working Just to Beef Up

Your Résumé Is Like Saving Up Sex for Your Old Age," *Business Insider*, November 11, 2015, http://goo.gl/W1wUBk.

17. "About," Social Enterprise Club, n.d., http://goo.gl/YBbBMi, accessed May 31, 2016; Net Impact, https://goo.gl/qUvG6u, accessed May 31, 2016.

18. S. Beckert and S. Rockman, "How Slavery Led to Modern Capitalism: Echoes," Bloomberg, January 24, 2012.

CHAPTER 3: THE LIMITS OF IMPACT INVESTMENT

1. "Migration Grant Guidelines," MacArthur Foundation, n.d., http://goo.gl/ars8du, accessed January 20, 2017.

2. Max Pichulik, "NexThought Monday—Impact White Washing? When Any Deal in a Developing Country with a Few Generic Metrics Can Be Considered Impactful," Next Billion, n.d., http://goo.gl/TWj9Tp.

3. Joshua D. Rhodes, "When Will Rooftop Solar Be Cheaper Than the Grid? Here's a Map," The Conversation, n.d., http://goo.gl/W4slj0.

4. N. O'Donohoe, C. Leijonhufvud, Y. Saltuk, A. Bugg-Levine, and M. Brandenburg, *Impact Investments: An Emerging Asset Class*, J. P Morgan Global Research, The Rockefeller Foundation, and Global Impact Investment Network, November 29, 2010, http://goo.gl/5PTAUs, accessed January 20, 2017.

5. INCITE! Women of Color Against Violence, *The Revolution Will Not Be Funded: Beyond the Non-Profit Industrial Complex* (Cambridge, MA: South End Press, 2007).

6. See Amy Huffman, "Freada Kapor Klein: Genius Is Equally Distributed by Zip Code, Opportunity Is Not," Exitevent, September 14, 2016, http://goo.gl/465sKA.

7. "How Many People Live in California," Suburban Stats, n.d., https://goo.gl/FBDxM8, accessed July 2, 2016.

8. "Here's a Detailed Breakdown of Racial and Gender Diversity Data Across U.S. Venture Capital Firms," *Techcrunch*, October 6, 2015, https://goo.gl/v11fn7, accessed July 2, 2016.

CHAPTER 4: SCALING SMART

1. N. O'Donohoe, C. Leijonhufvud, Y. Saltuk, A. Bugg-Levine, and M. Brandenburg, *Impact Investments: An Emerging Asset Class*, J. P Morgan Global Research, The Rockefeller Foundation, and Global Impact Investment Network, November 29, 2010, http://goo.gl/5PTAUs, accessed January 20, 2017.

2. J. Militzet, "The Impact of Tech: Sandhya Hegde of Khosla Impact Fund Discusses How High-Tech Solutions Can Transform Lives at the BoP," Next Billion, November 5, 2015, htpp://goo.gl/saKYJ3, accessed January 20, 2017.

3. R. Rosenberg, "CGAP Reflections on the Compartamos Initial Public Offering," Consultative Group to Assist the Poor (CGAP), June 1, 2007, http://goo.gl/bYjm1z, accessed January 20, 2017.

4. Development Initiatives, *Investments to End Poverty: Real Money, Real Choices, Real Lives*, 2013, http://goo.gl/aUN3jG, accessed January 20, 2017; S. Strom and V. Bajaj, "Rich I.P.O. Brings Controversy to SKS Microfinance," *New York Times*, July 29, 2010.

5. M. M. Pitt and S. R. Khandker, "The Impact of Group-Based Credit Programs on Poor Households in Bangladesh: Does the Gender of Participants Matter?," *Journal of Political Economy* 106, no. 5 (1998): 958–996; D. Roodman and J. Morduch, "The Impact of Microcredit on the Poor in Bangladesh: Resisting Evidence," Center for Global Development, 2009, http://goo.gl/vQcRdd.

6. K. Odell, *Measuring the Impact of Microfinance* (Washington, DC: Grameen Foundation, 2010).

7. M. Yunus, "Sacrificing Microcredit for Megaprofits," *New York Times*, January 14, 2011.

8. N. Macfarquhar, "Banks Making Big Profits from Tiny Loans," *New York Times*, April 13, 2010.

9. M. Yunus, "Social Business," Yunus Centre, December 25, 2007, http://goo.gl/OLX35v, accessed June 6, 2016.

10. "Grameen Crédit Agricole Fund: A Lever for Development," Grameen Crédit Agricole Fund, n.d., http://goo.gl/tw1DmL, accessed February 4, 2017.

CHAPTER 6: ENGAGING COMMUNITIES

1. "Rio Favela Facts," Catalytic Communities (CatComm), http://goo.gl/KTdQWL, accessed February 13, 2017.

2. R. DiAngelo, "White Fragility," *International Journal of Critical Pedagogy* 3, no. 3 (2011): 54–70.

3. R. Rosenberg, "CGAP Reflections on the Compartamos Initial Public Offering," Consultative Group to Assist the Poor (CGAP), June 1, 2007, http://goo.gl/bYjm1z, accessed January 20, 2017.

4. Octavio Vélez Ascencio, in NoticiasNet.mx, quoted in Selene Aparicio (trans.), "The 'Dark Side' of Wind Power in Mexico," *Renewable Energy Mexico*, May 4, 2012, http://goo.gl/TxMsK5, accessed January 20, 2017.

5. J. A. Schertow, "Solidarity with the Resistance Against Corporate Windfarm in Oaxaca, Mexico," *Intercontinental Cry*, November 5, 2012, http://goo.gl/lq9XF4, accessed January 20, 2017.

CHAPTER 7: ADDING MORE VALUE THAN YOU EXTRACT

1. J. Hornbeck, "The Argentine Financial Crisis: A Chronology of Events," Congressional Research Service, Library of Congress, January 31, 2002.

2. C. Zimring and W. Rathje, *Encyclopedia of Consumption and Waste: The Social Science of Garbage* (Thousand Oaks, CA: SAGE Publications, 2012).

3. B. Dangl, "Occupy, Resist, Produce: Worker Cooperatives in Argentina," *Upside Down World*, March 6, 2005, http://goo.gl/su7brm.

4. "Our Mission," The Working World, 2016, http://goo.gl /isDEYW, accessed July 2, 2016.

5. K. Vellinger, M. Simon, and S. Oceransky, *Redefining Impact: Case Studies in Transformative Finance*, Toniic and The Transformative Finance Network, 2013, http://goo.gl/1rcrma, accessed January 20, 2017.

6. "Loans," The Working World, n.d., http://goo.gl/OTl0eL, accessed July 2, 2016.

CHAPTER 8: BALANCING RISK AND RETURN

1. Cocoa Barometer, 2015, http://goo.gl/oGgyEV, accessed January 20, 2017.

2. "History of Fairtrade," Fairtrade International, 2011, http://goo.gl /Bfs3lm, accessed June 14, 2016; "What Is Fairtrade," Fairtrade International, 2011, http://goo.gl/Bfs3lm, accessed June 14, 2016.

3. C. Doutre-Roussel, *The Chocolate Connoisseur: For Everyone with a Passion for Chocolate* (London: Piatkus Books, 2005).

4. "Emily Stone," Ashoka Innovators for the Public, 2014, http://goo .gl/nQLoEd, accessed June 14, 2016.

5. *The World Factbook*, Central Intelligence Agency, http://goo .gl/gA2RHt, accessed January 20, 2017; *2009 Country Poverty Assessment*, National Human Development Advisory Committee, Ministry of Economic Development, Commerce and Industry, and Consumer Protection, Belize, August 2010.

6. "Indigenous Innovation: Revolutionizing Cacao Production in Belize," Kickstarter, 2014, https://goo.gl/OBeVqt, accessed June 14, 2016.

7. "Facts and Figures," Specialty Coffee Association of America, http:// goo.gl/moumvX, accessed June 14, 2016.

CHAPTER 9: MAXIMIZING IMPACT

1. "IRIS: The Rockefeller Foundation," Global Impact Investing Network, n.d., https://goo.gl/luiyu4, accessed June 12, 2017.

2. "GIIRS Ratings," B Analytics, 2016, http://goo.gl/HeoEtW, accessed June 12, 2016.

3. World Bank, *IFC Jobs Study: Assessing Private Sector Contributions to Job Creation and Poverty Reduction* (Washington, DC: World Bank Group, January 2013, http://goo.gl/oppggh, accessed January 20, 2017.

4. "Fight Poverty: Move the GDP Needle," Endeavor, September 17, 2012, http://goo.gl/3TsijO, accessed June 12, 2015.

5. A. Lowrey, "Income Inequality May Take Toll on Growth," *New York Times*, October 16, 2012.

6. International Labour Organization, *World Employment and Social Outlook 2016*, January 2016, http://goo.gl/yBhgiE, accessed February 13, 2017.

7. G. S. Fields, *Working Hard, Working Poor: A Global Journey* (New York: Oxford University Press, 2012).

8. C. DeNavas-Walt and B. Proctor, *Income and Poverty in the United States*, US Department of Commerce, US Census Bureau (Washington DC: US Government Printing Office, 2012); L. Sullivan, T. Meschede, L. Dietrich, and T. Shapiro, *The Racial Wealth Gap: Why Policy Matters*, Institute for Assets and Social Policy, Brandeis University, and Demos, 2015, http://goo.gl/n2X5w6, accessed January 20, 2017.

9. "L&J: About Us," Liberty and Justice, n.d., http://goo.gl/BDkAeA, accessed June 13, 2016.

10. Huntington Capital, "2013 Annual Impact Report: Pioneering High Performance Impact Investing," 2013, http://goo.gl/Ewc9Ek; see also "About SBA," Small Business Administration, n.d., https://goo.gl/A0pNYQ, accessed June 14, 2016.

11. See Jobs with Justice, www.jwj.org, accessed June 14, 2016; Berkeley Labor Center, http://laborcenter.berkeley.edu, accessed June 14, 2016; For Working Families, www.forworkingfamilies.org, accessed June 14, 2016.

12. E. Appelbaum, R. Milkman, L. Elliott, and T. Kroeger, *Good for Business? Connecticut's Paid Sick Leave Law*, Center for Economic and Policy Research, 2014, http://goo.gl/ceHGtv.

13. "Paid Sick Days: Good for Business, Good for Workers," National Partnership for Women & Families, August 2012, http://goo.gl/cxQ8q9.

14. W. Cascio, "The High Cost of Low Wages," *Harvard Business Review*, December 2006.

15. C. X. Chen and T. Sandino, "Can Wages Buy Honesty? The Rela-

tionship Between Relative Wages and Employee Theft," CtW Investment Group, n.d., http://goo.gl/RkRsDa.

16. D. Kruse, "Research Evidence on Prevalence and Effects of Employee Ownership: 2002 Report by Douglas Kruse, Rutgers University," Testimony Before the Subcommittee on Employer-Employee Relations, Committee on Education and the Workforce, US House of Representatives, February 13, 2002, posted at National Center for Employee Ownership, http://goo.gl/laAYwO, accessed February 13, 2017.

CHAPTER 10: REAL IMPACT AT SCALE

1. *Establishing Long Term Value and Performance*, Deutsche Bank Group, 2012, http://goo.gl/Fyvj3G, accessed February 4, 2017; *The Impact of Corporate Sustainability on Organizational Processes and Performance*, Harvard Business School, 2010, http://goo.gl/MP1v3V, accessed February 4, 2017.

2. "Transform Finance Investor Network Launches at White House with $556 Million Pledge," Philanthropy New York, June 25, 2014, https://goo.gl/aEcLfX, accessed July 2, 2016; "Background on the White House Roundtable on Impact Investing," White House, n.d., https://goo.gl/dcSN91, accessed July 2, 2016.

3. *Internal Revenue Manual*, IRS, 2016, https://goo.gl/XdwwDr, accessed June 3, 2016.

CHAPTER 11: WHAT YOU CAN DO

1. "Weekly National Rates and Rate Caps," Federal Deposit Insurance Corporation, http://goo.gl/9j5A6P, accessed June 14, 2016.

2. "Featured CD," Bank of America, n.d., http://goo.gl/uPR624, accessed June 14, 2016.

3. "Impact Savings and Money Market," New Resource Bank, n.d., http://goo.gl/Y6oLc9, accessed June 14, 2016.

4. *Establishing Long Term Value and Performance*, Deutsche Bank Group, 2012, http://goo.gl/Fyvj3G, accessed February 4, 2017.

5. *The Impact of Corporate Sustainability on Organizational Processes and Performance*, Harvard Business School, 2011, http://goo.gl/MP1v3V, accessed February 4, 2017.

6. K. Begos and J. Loviglio, "College Fossil-Fuel Divestment Movement Builds," Yahoo News, May 23, 2013, http://goo.gl/H4f9Xs, accessed February 4, 2017.

7. First Affirmative, www.firstaffirmative.com, accessed June 14, 2016.

8. S. Merkel, "What Is the Difference Between a ROTH, SEP and Traditional IRA?" Investopedia, http://goo.gl/XqINxS, accessed June 14, 2016.

9. Homeboy Industries, www.homeboyindustries.org, accessed June 14, 2016.

10. National Domestic Workers Alliance, www.domesticworkers.org, accessed June 14, 2016.

11. Restaurants Opportunities Centers United, http://rocunited.org, accessed June 14, 2016.

12. National Association for Latino Community Asset Builders, www.nalcab.org, accessed June 14, 2016.

13. Transform Finance, http://transformfinance.org, accessed June 14, 2016.

14. Accelerate Change, http://acceleratechange.org, accessed June 14, 2016.

15. The Workers Lab, http://theworkerslab.com, accessed June 14, 2016.

16. Uncharted Institute, http://uncharted.org, accessed June 14, 2016.

17. "GSBI Programs," Miller Center for Social Entrepreneurship, www.scu-social-entrepreneurship.org/gsbi, accessed February 4, 2017.

18. Village Capital, www.vilcap.com, accessed June 14, 2016.

19. SMASHD Labs, http://smashdlabs.co, accessed February 4, 2017.

20. International Accountability Project, http://accountabilityproject.org, accessed June 14, 2016.

21. P. Salkin and A. Lavine, "Negotiating for Social Justice and the Promise of Community Benefits Agreements: Case Studies of Current and Developing Agreements," *Journal of Affordable Housing & Community Development Law* 17 (2008): 113–144.

CONCLUSION: ASKING QUESTIONS

1. Israel Shenker, "E. B. White: Notes and Comment by Author," *New York Times*, July 11, 1969, http://goo.gl/EuRVX, accessed January 20, 2017.

INDEX

Javier Machado

Morgan Simon is a widely recognized leader in impact investment who builds bridges between finance and social justice. Over the past seventeen years, she has influenced over $150 billion from high-net-worth individuals, foundations, and endowments. She supports Pi Investments and the Libra Foundation, and is also co-founder and chair of the nonprofit Transform Finance.

Previously, she served as the founding CEO of Toniic, a global network of impact investors, and as the founding executive director of the Responsible Endowments Coalition. She has also worked with the United Nations in Honduras, in corporate reform with ForestEthics, and in domestic microfinance with the Women's Initiative for Self-Employment. She currently serves on the boards of the Restaurant Opportunities Centers (ROC), The Working World, and CARE Enterprises. A graduate of Swarthmore College, Simon serves as an adjunct professor at Middlebury College's graduate school program. She lives in the Bay Area.

Simon can be reached at www.morgansimon.com.

The Nation Institute

NATION
BOOKS

Founded in 2000, **Nation Books** has become a leading voice in American independent publishing. The imprint's mission is to tell stories that inform and empower just as they inspire or entertain readers. We publish award-winning and bestselling journalists, thought leaders, whistleblowers, and truthtellers, and we are also committed to seeking out a new generation of emerging writers, particularly voices from underrepresented communities and writers from diverse backgrounds. As a publisher with a focused list, we work closely with all our authors to ensure that their books have broad and lasting impact. With each of our books we aim to constructively affect and amplify cultural and political discourse and to engender positive social change.

Nation Books is a project of The Nation Institute, a nonprofit media center established to extend the reach of democratic ideals and strengthen the independent press. The Nation Institute is home to a dynamic range of programs: the award-winning Investigative Fund, which supports groundbreaking investigative journalism; the widely read and syndicated website TomDispatch; journalism fellowships that support and cultivate over twenty-five emerging and high-profile reporters each year; and the Victor S. Navasky Internship Program.

For more information on Nation Books and The Nation Institute, please visit:

www.nationbooks.org
www.nationinstitute.org
www.facebook.com/nationbooks.ny
Twitter: @nationbooks